# THE WEST END WAREHO[USE]
## 286 to 302, Sauchiehall St., Glasg[ow]

### THE FASHION HOU[SE]

N COSTUME

TINGUE M

Fresh examples of the most recent developments o[f]
received from Paris, Berlin, London, &c., almost every
The WEST END WAREHOUSE was established
with a view to showing at how very moderate prices the
most fashionable Drapery and Millinery could be sold
appreciation of this scheme displayed b[y]
West of Scotland has emphatically st[ated]
the most successful of modern days

### Millinery.

cession of superlative and exquisit[e]
the foremost artistes in Paris and L[ondon]
can be added without being immed[iately]
Resident buyers in Paris and L[ondon]
dvantages quite unknown to thos[e]
wice a year.
thing new every time yo[u]

### [Mant]les.

[WEST END WAREHOUS]E has achieved a re[putation]
ot exceeded by any e[stablishment]
se out every underwe[ar]
our Mantle Rooms the
discount from the p[rice]

ghout the Season.

### [Evening a]nd Ball Dres[ses]

y of beautiful Costume[s]
favourite materials of
15 Pounds.

is, a pretty n[ovelty]

Wareh[ouse]

[SAUCHIEH]ALL STREE[T]

PRICE SIXPENCE.                                    COPYRIGHT.

# Illustrated Catalogue

### of the

## ORIGINAL COLLECTION

### of INSTRUMENTS of

# TORTURE

### from the

## Royal Castle of Nuremberg,

Amongst which will be found the Celebrated Original Iron

Maiden (Eiserne Jungfrau),

LENT FOR EXHIBITION BY

THE RIGHT HONOURABLE THE

## EARL OF SHREWSBURY AND TALBOT.

THIS CATALOGUE ARRANGED AND COMPILED,

AND THE COLLECTION CLASSIFIED AND DISPLAYED

BY

J. ICHENHÄUSER,

*Art Expert,*

68, NEW BOND STREET,

LONDON, W.

---

All communications regarding this Collection to be addressed to S. LEE BAPTY, F.R.G.S., &c., 3, Queen Victoria Street, London, E.C.

*Telegraphic Address*—"LEE BAPTY, LONDON."

# PREFACE.

## TORTURE.

"Man's inhumanity to man" plays such a leading part in the history of the World that it is impossible for us to discover at what period torture really began. Look where we will, undoubted evidence meets us of its existence in some shape or other. In Egypt, and later on in Athens, it was applied to slaves. The early Roman law only allowed it to be used in the case of slaves when examined as witnesses, or offenders, until the Christian Era, when, to propitiate their gods, and to try and stamp out the new religion, which was making such headway, the most barbarous and revolting tortures were resorted to. Nero, it is written, had many Christians sewn in the skins of wild animals, and then roasted slowly and horribly to death. Antoninius Pius had them scourged until their veins and sinews were laid bare; also, many were dismembered and torn asunder by wild horses.

Coming to the history of the more modern European countries, we find that in most German cities judicial torture was unknown until the end of the Fourteenth century, although it had existed in the statutes of the Italian Municipalities at a much earlier period. In most

European States it continued until the middle of the last century, when more enlightened views led to a general conviction of the inefficacy and injustice of this mode of ascertaining the truth. In France, the question *preparatoire* was discontinued in 1780, and torture in general was abolished throughout the French Dominions at the Revolution in 1789. In Russia its abolition, although recommended by the Empress Catherine in 1763, was not effected until 1801. In Austria, Prussia, and Saxony it was suspended soon after the middle of the last century, but, although seldom used, torture was allowed by the *laws of Bavaria and Hanover*, and some of the smaller German States, until *the end of the last century.*

In Scotland the use of torture was frequent until the reign of Queen Anne, when it was declared, by an Act for improving the union of the two kingdoms, "That in future no person accused of any crime in Scotland shall be subject or liable to any torture."

From the year 1468 until the Commonwealth, the practice of torture was very frequent in England. Particular instances are recorded in the Council books, and the Torture Warrants are still in existence. The last on record is 1640. The most terrible torture was known as the "*peine forte et dure*," which was peculiar to this country. It entailed the most fearful and agonizing suffering upon the victim. If the person charged refused to plead, he was condemned to the *peine forte et dure*, which was applied in this wise:—The victim was laid flat on his back, with his arms and legs drawn as far asunder as possible by ropes; then as much weight as he could bear was piled upon him, *and more.* This was increased day by day until he pleaded, or died. The very smallest possible amount of food was given, and the day he ate he was not allowed to drink. Who can picture the terrible suffering undergone by the unhappy wretch? And this was ordered in the name of religion or justice! For many years English writers and judges of high character condemned torture as contrary to the English Law; but, although this may have been acknowledged as not lawful in the ordinary sense, it was done under the prerogative of the Crown, which authorized this mode of discovering crimes which affected the State, such as treason or sedition, acting quite independently of the common law. This view of the subject is confirmed by the fact that in all instances of the application of torture, the warrants were issued immediately by the King or the Privy Council. The consequence was that in no country was torture as dangerous an instrument as in England, excepting perhaps in Spain, where, under the rule of the Holy Inquisition, the most inhuman and horrible atrocities were practised.

# THE RENOWNED COLLECTION
OF
# INSTRUMENTS OF TORTURE
From the Royal Castle of Nuremberg.

NUREMBERG, the old Reichstadt, the cradle of the Hohenzollerns, the birth-place of many of the fine arts, has a history which dates back to the earliest times. One of its oldest monuments is the burg or castle, of which the five-cornered tower existed in the days of the heathen. Here for many years this collection of torture instruments was an object of interest, not only to the inhabitants of the town, but to all travellers whose wanderings brought them that way. No journey to Bavaria could be counted completed until the burg had been visited and the "Iron Maiden" interviewed. The fiendish ingenuity displayed in the constructing of these instruments, so that they should inflict the greatest amount of suffering, shows that the question of torture must have not only been well thought out, but that it must have had the sanction and, if we may use the term, patronage of the law makers and municipalities. As we look through this collection, we see that neither tender youth, weak old age, delicate female, or ailing man was spared its horrors or its shame. And we cannot be too thankful to think we live in an age where more enlightened and humanitarian principles prevail.

This collection, so complete, may be to many somewhat gruesome, but it is of the *highest educational value*, as showing us the great strides which this century has made, not only in arts and sciences, but in the interests of truth, humanity, and justice. No more does the *Iron Maiden* clasp her unhappy and unwilling victim in her deadly embrace; no more are men and women broken on the *wheel,* tortured on the *rack*, branded with *red-hot irons*, driven mad with *thumb-screws*, stretched on *ladders*, or suffer the terrible and lingering *"peine forte et dure"*; and never again will the laws allow tender women to be mutilated by the horrible and sharp-clawed *spider*. These and hundreds of other instruments of the greater tortures will be found catalogued hereafter. For the punishments of lesser degrees or shame tortures, as great an amount of ingenuity is also evident. Shame masks and stocks for scolds; masks and cages for fraudulent tradesmen; for drunkards and brawlers, the drunkards' mantle, various masks, stocks, branding irons, collars, bracelets. For thieves and thief-children there are also torture instruments of various designs, all cruel and pitiless.

Religious or penitential torture is very rich in examples. Here we find branding irons, for burning on foreheads and backs; martyr lashes, which at every stroke tear away the flesh; pear-shaped screw gags, which entirely prevented any cries or exclamations; iron-spiked collars; torture seats; feet squeezers; iron boots, which were filled with hot water or molten metal; thumb-screws, &c., &c.

The executioner's axe or sword ended all torture, and no doubt in many cases came as a happy relief. Space forbids our enlarging further upon this interesting subject. To the student of bygone generations, and their cruelty in the dispensation of justice, we commend an inspection of the **torture instruments** catalogued herein.

IMPORTANT NOTICE.—*The Public is respectfully informed that this Collection is the only true and original one which was for so many years one of the sights of Nuremberg, where it was located in the Royal Castle.*

# CATALOGUE.

1 **Heavy Iron Shackle and Long Chain** for fastening prisoner up to a wall.
2 **An Old Roman Pair of Martyr Pincers, or Flesh Tearers.**
3 **Mouth-opener,** with gradations, to open a mouth to a certain size. Was used to slit the tongues of blasphemers.
4 **Pair of Iron Wrist Holders** for securing prisoners.
5 **Perforated Spoon or Sieve,** through which boiling water, oil, or molten lead was poured on to various portions of the body.
6 **Long Iron Gallows Screw.**
7 **Iron Brank,** with eyebrows, moustache, and three iron bars, worn by a parricide.
8 **Iron Body Ring,** with chains and hook to fasten up the criminal in a public place.
9 **Iron Crown** studded with round knobs, worn by Christian martyrs on their way to the auto-da-fé.
10 **Spanish Gaiter for Torturing the Leg,** with very formidably uneven shinbone presser.
11 **Branding Iron** from Bayreuth, with letter B.
12 **Long Gallows Screw.**
13 **Iron Spoon** for boiling pitch or tar, which was dropped through the perforations on to the naked body of the victim.

## Catalogue of Instruments of Torture, etc.

14 **An extra long Iron Chain** with shackle at one end, and padlock at the other.
15 **Pair of Hand Fasteners or Iron Bracelets.**
16 **Strong Venetian Iron Collar** with high iron crown and letter S (sacrilege).
17 **Strong Iron Manacle and Long Chain.**
18 **Pair of Iron Thumb-screws.**
19 **Shame Mask or Brank of Iron.** Devil's head painted, with movable tongue. For punishment of scolds.
20 **Broad Spanish Wrought Iron Collar** filled with sharp iron spikes.
21 **Similar Iron Spiked Collar.**
22 **Small Iron Collar,** covered with leather.
23 **Similar Neck Iron,** with bell and padlock. (See engraving, No. 1015).
24 **Heavy Iron Shackle with Chain.**
25 **Iron Thumbscrew.**
26 **Strong Iron Manacle and Long Chain.**
27 **Similar Iron Manacle and Chain.**
28 **Long Gallows Rope,** with hook at one end and pulley at the other.
29 **Iron Shame Mask or Brank,** painted, with long ass's ears, for drunkards or lazy ne'er-do-wells.
30 **Large-sized Strong Prison Padlock.**
31 **Flagellant of Iron-wire,** with spiked ends to tear the flesh.
32 **Heavy Iron Chain,** flagellants with five iron lashes.
33 **Curious Bronze Double Cross,** with inscription. This cross was supposed to have been used by witches when invoking their charms and incantations against anyone they were bewitching or overlooking.

## Catalogue of Instruments of Torture, etc.

34 **A Large Iron Mouth Opener**, used to fix the tongue before cutting it out.

35 **An Iron Implement**, affixed when Cutting off the Tongue.

36 **Double Scolds' Collar of Wood**, in which two women were fixed facing each other, hands and neck fastened, and so marched round the town.

37 **Iron Spoon** for melting lead, which was dropped on the naked bodies of the victims.

38 **Old Roman Martyr Pincers** With these terrible tongs or pincers were culprits and Christian martyrs tortured. Not only did they pinch the skin, or flay, but entire pieces of flesh were pulled away with them from the ribs. In the old Roman days they were known as "Ungula," and the early Germans knew them as "*Klaue*," because of their roughened or teeth-like appearance.

38a **An old book on Martyrdom and Torture**, with illustration of these Pincers and descriptions of their use.

39 **Condemned's Crucifix.** Crucifix made of wood, which the condemned criminal carried in his hand on his way to execution.

40 **Pair of Iron early Handcuffs or Wristlets**, with lock fastening.

41 **Cruel Iron Flagellant**, with five woven iron tails, each studded with a sharp spur-shaped star to cut into the flesh.

42 **A Jointed Iron Handcuff**, by which the wrists were fastened together.

43 **Strong Iron Double Hand-fastener and Thumbscrew** combined.

## Catalogue of Instruments of Torture, etc.

44 **An Iron Implement** affixed to the ears before they were cut off.

45 **Strong Iron Body Ring,** with long centre chain and a couple of strong iron wrist-fasteners.

46 **A Pair of Finger-screws.**

47 **Handscrew,** with coarsely roughened plank, so as to hurt the hands as much as possible.

48 **Iron Gallows Hook.**

49 **Extra Strong Wrought-iron Spiked Collar** studded with spikes inside and out.

50 **Iron Mail Chain Foot-glove** which was placed on the foot when red hot.

51 **A Similar Instrument.**

52 **A Branding Iron** from Bamberg for marking the letter B.

53 **Large Pair of Iron Martyr Tongs** for tearing the flesh.

54 **Large Ball-shaped Iron Ladle,** into which boiling oil was poured and then dropped on to the body through the perforations.

55 **A Pair of Manacles** with strong iron bar between, by which a prisoner was fastened to a horse.

56 **Spanish Wrought-iron Collar,** completely studded with sharp spikes inside and out.

57 **Branding Iron** which marked the letter U.

58 **Strong Iron Body Belt** with long iron chain and the side chain fixers to fasten to wall or to a running horse.

59 **An Early Spanish Pair-hand Handcuffs** with lock fastening.

## Catalogue of Instruments of Torture, etc. 13

60 **A somewhat similar one** of different formation, early Italian.

61 **Early German Copper Mask, Devil's Head and Horns,** all embossed with small heads over the nose, mouth and eyes, typical of a slanderous backbiting personage.

62 **A somewhat similar same-period Copper Mask,** likewise with small embossed face on end of nose.

63 **A somewhat similar Mask,** but with frog's eyes.

64 **Curious Iron Brank,** shape of devil's head, with stumpy horns, and small faces on the nose and cheeks, and with trumpet ears, for listeners, backbiters, &c.

65 **Strong Wooden Roller,** which was placed on the rack or on the stretching gallows, and over which the victim was rolled and stretched.

66 **Mask worn by the Judge of the notorious Vehmgericht,** of copper, pierced with five breathing holes, also with small perforations all round the edge so as to permit of a leather or cotton cap being sewn on.

As is well known, the accused before the Vehmgericht (secret judgment) did not see his judges. All were masked completely, the head being covered with a cap, and the face with such a mask as here shown. The accused may have been before his dearest friend, brother, or father, but he could not tell; and so sacred was the judge's oath, and so strong the influence exercised by the awe-inspiring tribunal, whose inexorable judgment none might gainsay, that the judges themselves dared not reveal their identity.

67 **Scold's Wooden Collar,** with two places for the hands. See note below.

68 **A somewhat similar Collar,** with four places for hands used for a man and his wife.

> NOTE.—Mr. William Andrews, in his interesting book, *Old Time Punishments*, says :—"Scolding women in the olden times were treated as offenders against the public peace, and for their transgressions were subjected to several cruel modes of punishment. The Corporations of towns during the middle ages made their own regulations for punishing persons guilty of crimes which were not rendered penal by the laws of the land. The punishments for correcting scolds differed greatly in various parts of the country. The free use of the tongue gave rise to riots and feuds to such an extent that it is difficult for us to realize at the present day."

69 **Long Wooden Roller,** studded with spikes, and known as a "spiked hare," used on the rack.

70 **A similar Roller,** with raised edges.

71 **Scold's Pillory,** shape of a violin, made of wood. In this the woman charged with being a scold was affixed, and so driven round the town, or whipped at the cart's tail, accompanied by the public executioner, or a drummer, who beat his drum to call the public's attention.

72 A ditto, somewhat longer.

73 **Scold's Collar of Oak,** in the shape of a ruff. This was fitted round the neck, and had to be worn as shame or penitence punishment for a certain time in a public place.

74 **Spanish Iron Collar,** studded inside with iron spikes, and with sharp saw-toothed edges, worn by religious martyrs.

75 **A very similar Iron Collar.**

76 **Malefactor's Collar Pillory**, with places for both hands. Made of wood, with very broad collar board so as to show out well in a crowded market-place or church porch.

77 A ditto, smaller, with sexagonal rim.

78 A ditto, round edge, with notched ornamentation.

79 **An Executioner's Sword** from the town of Bamberg, the guard embossed in representations of the Passions, wire-woven guard, to prevent it from slipping through the executioner's hand, and sharp double-edged blade.

80 **Headsman's Sword** from Nördlingen, with iron grip, engraved with gallows and wheel on the shield, also three perforations typical of the Holy Trinity and Armourer's mark.

81 **Small Iron Memento Mori**, worn with a chain round the neck on the way to execution.

82 **A Pair of early Iron Handcuffs** fastened with chain.

83 **Executioner's Sword.** Belonging to the Nuremberg Executioner, Franz Schmidt. It has a gilt metal top and guard. On the side of the blade are the following verses:—

> Die Herrn steuern dem Unheil
> Und ich executire das Urtheil
> Wenn ich das Schwerdt thu aufheben
> So geb Gott dem armen Sünder das ewige Leben.

TRANSLATION.—The world steers towards mischief, and I execute the judgment When I lift up my sword, God give the poor sinner eternity.

84 **Executioner's Extra Heavy Sword**, with sharp-pointed blade, straight long guard and wire-covered hilt, strong iron-pointed ferrule top.

**85 Executioner's Sword**, Thuringen executioner, Balthasar Glaser, 1742, with gilt metal work, and the motto:—

> Hüte Dich, Thu kein Böses nicht,
> So Kommst du nicht ins Gericht.

TRANSLATION.—Be careful, do no ill, and you won't come to judgment.

Under the verses are engraved, "Justice & St. Michael." On the handle is the letter "G," and it bears the name of owner and date (1742).

**86 An Extra Long and Extra Strong Iron Chain**, with foot shackle at one end and strong iron bar to fasten on to a wall at the other end.

**87 A Heavy Hempen Scourge or Whip**, with numerous lashes, each one having a steel barb woven into it so as to cut at each stroke.

**88 A similar one, not so heavy.**

It was a common thing in England for prisoners to be whipped with a three-cord whip knotted at each end, and in the feudal times servants were often whipped to death. Whipping vagrants at the cart's tail was also greatly resorted to, and in many a country town or village a whipping-post exists until this day. In the penetential cell the scourge was also greatly used, and from what we can gather was of the utmost severity. Many of the whips and rods in this collection seem to be of unusual strength, and were doubtless used by the public executioner on criminals without the slightest mercy.

**89 Long Spiked Wooden Roller**, with numerous rows of long spikes. Known as a "spiked hare." The victim was laid on a bench or stretched on a ladder, and the "spiked hare" was rolled over his naked body, or, to vary it, he was rolled over the spikes. Some of the old writers describe this torture as being most fearful.

## Catalogue of Instruments of Torture, etc.

**90 Thief-catcher.** Very curious instrument, was used with a long wooden handle, terminating at the top with a round hoop, garnished inside with triangular iron spikes. The front of the hoop is made to push open, so that the officer of the law can push it round the neck, arm, or leg of whoever he wants to catch, who on his or her part has no possible means of getting away, the ring having closed on him and preventing any effort to escape.

**91 Iron Manacle.**

**92 Manacle,** somewhat similar.

**93 A Pair of Wrist-fasteners,** each at the end of a long iron bar so as to keep the arms wide apart; were used when prisoners were being whipped.

**94 Similar Instrument,** somewhat shorter, with two padlocks.

**95 Very Powerful Spiked Hare,** with sharp iron spikes. When the victim was rolled over this terrible instrument he was completely impaled and disembowelled.

**96 Strong Coupling-iron,** with manacle at each end to fasten two people.

**97 Large Heavy Hand Axe,** with metal grip, used to cut off the right-hand of those convicted of treason or parricides.

**98 Headsman's Sword** from Bayreuth, with brass grip, and with the motto:—

"Ich stehe hoff nebst Gott zu richten recht,
Jesus du bist der Richter und ich der Knecht."

TRANSLATION.—"I stand under God to execute aright,
Jesus, Thou art the Judge and I the servant."

under this a figure of Justice and some ornamentation; also:—

"O Herr nimm Diesen Sünder auff in dein Reich,
Damit er kann werden vor einem glücklichen streich."

TRANSLATION.—"Oh, God, take this sinner into Thy Kingdom,
That he may know happiness."

under this a knight with dagger, and some ornamentation.

B

## Catalogue of Instruments of Torture, etc.

99 **Executioner's Sword** from Munich, with iron guard shagreen handle, in leather sheath and original belt. On the blade is damascened in gold a man being beheaded and St. George, also the verses as per Nos. 233 and 272.

100 **Headsman's Sword** from Augsburg with extra long and straight guard, the hilt of leather wound round with wire to keep it from slipping.

101 **A Pair of Iron Bracelets** with aperture to fix on to a chain.

102 **A somewhat similar Pair of Handcuffs**, with lock and key.

103 **Iron Brank or Shame Mask**, with ass's ears and painted face, from Regensburg, worn by drunkards.

104 **A similar Iron Mask** worn by females.

105 **Iron Crown**, with interior four-cornered knobs to press on the head. Was used for females.

106 **Relief Carved Portrait**, in wood, of the Nuremburg hangman of the year 1578. Very characteristic.

107 **Foot Padlock.** An instrument in which the feet were locked, as holding them tighter than a chain, when the culprit was placed in a frequented spot loose or fastened to a wall or tree.

108 **Iron Mail Chain Glove**, was made red hot before being put on.

109 **A similar Mail Glove.**

110 \* **Hiesel's Gun**, a very heavy and massive arm with very large bore, the stock so arranged by Hiesel himself that he could fire it off from either shoulder. The lock was also engraved by him.

\* Hiesel was a notorious bandit who lived about the end of last century, and whose name spread terror

*Catalogue of Instruments of Torture, etc.* 19

through all the hill-lands of Upper Bavaria. For many years he was able to elude the vigilant hunt made for him by the soldiery or police, but at last he was taken and executed.

**111 Strong Iron Foot Presser or Foot Screw**, the cruelty of which is apparent.

**112 Set of Irons**, consisting of two strong iron bands, two shackles, a pair of handcuffs, padlock, small weights, and twelve-link chain ; with this a police officer was enabled to couple a pair of prisoners.

**113 A strong Iron Leg Shackle, long Chain and Padlock**, used for chaining prisoner in a dungeon.

**114 Long Iron Bar**, with manacle at each end, was used at the whipping post.

**115 Similar One** with ornamental iron bar.

**116 A small Iron Thumb-screw**, early Italian.

**117 A similar Thumb-screw.**

**118 Executioner's Sword**, belonging to the last headsman of Nuremburg, beautifully damascened blade, the armourer's mark and inscription, straight guard and wire-woven hilt.

**119 A Dutch Executioner's Sword**, with strongly ribbed blade and leather hilt.

**120 An Executioner's Sword**, from the Low Countries, strongly ribbed and pointed blade.

**121 Headsman's or Executioner's Sword**, from Eichstaedt, round pointed blade, wire hilt, long guard.

**122 Executioner's Sword** from Erlangen with shagreen scabbard, the blade engraved with " St. Michael & St. James," the date 1757, and with the following inscription: " Jesus Nazarenus Rex Judaeorum, 1737." and " Et verbum caro factum est.—I.H.S." Beyond which, the sword is beautifully ornamented.

123 **A Gallows Rope.**
124 **A similar Gallows Rope.**
125 **An unknown Fragment of a Sharp, Dangerous, Torture Instrument.**
126 **A Pair of Strongly Locked Handcuffs** fastened on to a long iron bar.
127 **Venetian Bandit's Dagger.**
128 **A similar Dagger,** smaller.
129 **Branding Iron,** marks the letter U.
130 **Another Branding Iron** from the Town of Fuerth, marking the letter F.
131 **A Gallows Mark Branding Iron.**
132 **Long Iron Whip,** black wood handle and three chain iron lashes; would not only tear the flesh, but break a bone when applied with force.
133 **Scold's Collar,** perfect fiddle shape, with following inscription:—
"Vor die schwatzhaft—und unzüchtigen Weiber zu Poen. Sirah Nagelnei Geigenmacher.—*Allerertn Wohnaft*, d. 28 *Jan.*, 1683.
For talkative and scolding women as a penitence.—Sirah Nagelnei, fiddlemaker, 28th Jany., 1683."
134 **Prison Warder's Weapon** in the shape of a hammer; strong wood handle and iron head for stunning a prisoner.
135 **A Jointed Chain Hand-fastener** to bind both hands together.
136 **An Iron Tongue Tearer** in the shape of a pair of tongs with screw. With this instrument a strong hold could be taken of a tongue so that it could be torn right out by the roots. Was used on blasphemers, heretics, &c., &c.
137 **An Iron Armlet and Lock Combined,** with inscription of maker's name.

## Catalogue of Instruments of Torture, etc.

138 **A Very Early Strong Iron Double Hand-Fastener** with lock and key.

139 **An Iron Whip** with six sharp-edged iron tails.

140 **Spanish Mouth-Pear, or Gag,** made of iron and in sections, so that it may be squeezed together in the shape of a pear (hence its name). This was used for those condemned to torture or those privately seized. The instrument was forced into the mouth and then, by touching the screw, it springs open, and the victim could utter no sound.

141 **An Iron Winder or Gallows Hook.**

142 **An Iron Winder or Gallows Hook,** larger.

143 Another.

144 **An Iron Gallows Screw.**

145 **A Strong Iron Gallows Swivel Screw.**

146 **A Constable's Staff** of heavy metal, the grip covered with leather, the end in the shape of a man's fist, a blow from which would break the hardest skull.

147 **Large Gag,** with wooden handle and with spring movement, so as to open when forced into the mouth. Spanish. This gag, although of a different formation from No. 140, was equally as effective in subduing all cries and in preventing any resistance on the part of the condemned.

148 **An Old English Executioner's Axe,** with date 1539, under which coat-of-arms with lettering, also the three indents which signify the Trinity.

149 **Executioner's Axe,** with long wooden handle and metal ferrule. French.

150 **Headsman's Sword,** from Ulm, with iron grip, long leather handle, with a wheel and a gallows inlaid in the blade.

151 **Curious Finger Axe**, heavy iron blade.
152 **A Venetian Executioner's Sword**, short, with brass grip; gallows and wheel on the blade.
153 **Large Leather Collar** of Hiesel's big dog, with large brass nails and owner's monogram.
154 **Pair of Manacles and a Shackle**, with thirty-jointed chain.
155 **A Scold's Wooden Collar**, with pillory for neck and both hands.
156 **Another**, very similar, iron bound.
157 **Heavy Iron Wire Penitential Rod.**
158 **Iron Whip**, with five iron wire lashes, each one with rows of spur-shaped spikes to cut into the flesh.
159 **A Penitential Iron Whip**, with twelve sharp-edged flat iron lashes.
160 **Iron Wire Whip**, with five lashes completely studded with iron spikes.
161 **Hempen Whip**, with six lashes and barbed wire ends.
162 **Very curious strong Prison Padlock**, early Spanish
163 **Neck Iron and Pair of Shackles**, with seventeen-link chain. The prisoner was fastened by the feet to the iron round his neck.
164 **Strong Neck Iron**, with padlock and double length iron chain.
165 **Iron Thumb-screw.**
166 **Another Thumb-screw** of different shape and stronger.
167 **An exceedingly powerful Pair of Iron Wrist-screws.**
168 **A Pair of Iron Handcuffs** or double bracelets.
169 **An Executioner's Rapier**, with silver guard. This sword was worn by the hangman on his right side.
170 **A Similar Sword**, with embossed guard and pommel, silver-mounted grip.

## Catalogue of Instruments of Torture, etc.

**171 Curious Wooden Devil's Head Mask,** with real goat's horns, for dishonest children.

**172 Hempen Whip,** with six thongs, for youthful offenders.

**173 Small Shackle and light Chain** for youths.

**174 A Manacle** with ten-linked chain for young people.

**175 Prison Warder's Weapon,** for self-defence, in the shape of a whip, with a heavy weight at the end. Short strong handle, with a twisted chain terminating in the weight.

**176 Mask,** worn by the poison mixer, Rudhart, of Stuttgart; made of leather and arranged with small holes over the mouth and nose for breathing purposes.

**177 A curious Double Scold's Collar** in which two women were pilloried, fastened necks and hands, and marched together thus involuntarily united round the town.

**178 Another,** somewhat similar.

**179 A very curious Wooden-handled Whip.**

**180 A Whip,** somewhat similar.

**181 Iron Prison** in the shape of a body ring, handcuffs, and foot shackles, with chain to fasten to a wall.

**182 A very long and extra strong Iron Chain,** with shackle and long iron security bar.

**183 Venetian Iron Collar,** with projecting rod terminating in a bell, so that the prisoner could not move without giving notice to the warders and watchers.

**184 A very curious and ponderous Iron Instrument,** so constructed as to hold feet, hands, and neck, keeping the prisoner suspended in a most painful and awkward position.

**185 A Venetian Iron Collar and Belt,** somewhat similar to No. 183.

**186 A Strong pair of Iron Wrist-pressers.**

187 A small pair of Finger-screws.
188 A Hempen Rod, with numerous lashes, each terminating in a spiked barb.
189 Another Hempen Rod, with knotted lashes.
190 Another, somewhat similar.
191 Belt of Chastity, with the symbol of love—a flaming heart pierced with two arrows—ornamented with green velvet and gold bordering of lace, constructed with double lock.
192 Belt of Chastity, sharp edged, and the ironwork jointed.
193 Belt of Chastity, somewhat similar, covered with red velvet.
194 Long Iron Flagellant, with five iron lashes completely studded with spikes and barbs.
195 Another Iron Whip, with six spur-shaped ends.
196 Strong Gallows Hook.
197 Another Iron Gallows Hook.
198 Another, larger and stronger.
199 A ditto, smaller.
200 A Long Iron Gallows Nail.
201 A Similar Screw, smaller.
202 Another.
203 A Long Straight Gallows Nail.
204 Thumbscrew of the oldest and most simple construction for the most painful pressing and screwing entirely through the thumb.
205 A Curious Pair of Thumb-Holders. The thumbs were fastened to this, and the culprit easily led along or fastened up in a public place; resistance was impossible.
206 A Pair of Manacles and Chains, completely confining both hands.

207 **Double Scolds' Collar.** In this the women who had quarrelled were placed, neck and hands, and were forced to stand thus facing each other until they were, or pretended to be, friends again.

208 **A Double Scolds' Collar,** somewhat different in shape and of a later date.

209 & 210 **Two Iron Manacles.**

211 **Strong Iron Pillory,** with places for the neck and hands, surmounted by a bell and a weathercock; worn by turncoats and unreliable people.

212 **A Penitent's Girdle,** made of barbed wire, which, when worn next to the flesh, caused the most unpleasant and uncomfortable irritation.

213 **A Long Iron Chain** for fastening up a prisoner securely. Heavy iron padlock at one end, strong ankle ring at the other.

214 **The Russian Knout,** made of bullets of lead, covered with leather, and strung together. With this terrible instrument slaves and prisoners of all kinds were scourged.

215 **Copper Boot,** which was filled with boiling water or molten lead.

216 **Another,** similar.

217 **A Hempen Whip** with six knotted lashes.

218 **Another** with very numerous lashes, spur-iron edges.

219 **A Pair of Wooden Pinching Shears** to pinch the fingers or toes.

220 **Iron Body Ring** with pair of hand bracelets and eleven-linked chain.

221 **Implement for fastening the Ankles together,** with place through which to fix an iron chain.

222 **Catgut Head-tormentor**, with iron handle for the executioner; with this he twisted the cords across the forehead until the victim was almost scalped.
223 **Iron Penitential Whip** with five sharp-edged iron tails.
224 **Very Powerful Screw Iron Foot Breaker or Toe Screw.** Entailed the most terrible pain.
225 **Powerful Iron Handscrew**, with differently roughened Base.

Who can tell the fearful torture of the thumbscrew, which was so freely used in all European countries? Was a man charged with any crime or supposed to know of any plot against the Church or the Government, the ordeal of the thumbscrew made him confess, even if he was innocent! It was not in human nature (except in *very rare cases*), to stand this ordeal long; and under its baneful influence, its heartbreaking torture, who knows how many perfectly innocent people were accused and convicted of crimes they had never thought of?

226 **Branding Iron** from Utretch, brands letter U.
227 **Branding Iron**, brands with mark of the gallows.
228 **Large Gallows Screw** from which the condemned was hanged.
229 **A curious Iron Cupping Machine**, with which letters or designs were burnt into the flesh.
230 **A Spiked Roller**, over which a man was rolled when on the rack.
231 **A Pair of Shackles and strong Chain.**
232 **Leather Head Halter**, which was placed on the head of the condemned and held by the executioner's assistant.

233 **Executioner's Sword** from Regeneburg, with engraved blade and motto:—
>Die Herrn steuren dem Unheil
>Ich exequire ihr End Urtheil

and a figure of Justice.

On the other side—
>Wann ich das Schwert thu aufheben
>Wünche ich dem Sünder das ewige Leben.

a figure of Justice and the date 1754, also the armourer's mark.

234 **Executioner's Sword** from Crailsheim Ellwangen Würtemberg, with broad blade.

235 **Executioner's Sword** from Brannenberg, in Upper Bavaria, with iron guard and strong swept blade and armourer's mark.

236 **Double Thumbscrew.**

237 **Another** somewhat similar.

238 **A curious Yoke.** This was worn by the father and mother of a child born out of wedlock. When yoked together they were forced to carry water up to the top of the hill, doubtless up into the old Castle of Nuremberg. (See engraving, No. 996).

239 **Long Chain of Nine Links**, with shackle or foot fastener.

240 **Another long Chain and a Shackle.**

241 **Curious Shame Mask or Brank**, female head worn by dishonest or immoral women.

242 **Very curious large Iron Brank or Mask**, with goggle-eyes, large open mouth, worn by blasphemers.

243 **Iron Mask**, with painted face, worn by youthful criminals.

244 **Curious pair of Iron Braces**, with front and back bars, body ring, and padlock, in which a man was tightly held, and had no power of resistance.

**245** A pair of round **Wrist-holders,** with lock and key.
**246** A similar pair, not so heavy.
**247** Strong Iron **Ankle Fasteners,** by which prisoner was secured so as not to be able to move unless released.
**248** A heavy **Iron Shackle** or **Leg Iron.**
**249** A painful double **Hand-screw,** constructed so that the whole ten fingers could be squeezed at the same time.
**250** A **Double-handed Headman's Sword,** extra long blade, with armourer's mark and sign of the Trinity.
**251** A **Military Executioner's Sword,** with princely and military ornamentation, as well as the three perforations (the Trinity) in the blade.
**252** An **Oriental Executioner's Sword,** with brass guard and hilt, ribbed blade, pointed end.
**253** Pair of **Handbracelets** or **Handcuffs,** with long chain and padlock.
**254** Another, somewhat the same.
**255** A **Gallows Rope.**
**256** Another **Gallows Rope.**
**257** A **Chain** to bind two prisoners by the ankles.
**258** Very Powerful Iron **Foot-presser** or **Foot-screw.**
**259** Another, somewhat different, with sharp internal spur-shaped screw to mutilate the foot.
**260** A **Penitent's Girdle,** made of iron wire, with sharp points to press into the flesh.
**261** Long **Iron Chain Whip,** with five thongs barbed.
**261a** **Iron Torture Stocks,** three feet high, with divisions for neck, hands, and feet. In consequence of the shape of these stocks, when a man's hands and neck were fastened the position was an exceedingly painful one.

*Catalogue of Instruments of Torture, etc.*

**261b A Pair of Iron Pincers,** which were made red-hot and so used. There were various different marks awarded in the punishment, and the victim had to be burned so many times an hour. For each time he branded, the executioner received a certain fee.

**262 Tongue-tearer.** A pair of tongs so arranged with screws and sharp teeth that it took a firm grip of the tongue. Used on blasphemers.

**263 Similar Pair of Tongue-tearers,**

**264 Iron Spider.** This instrument, somewhat like a spider, with long sharp claws, was used to grip the flesh of various portions of the body and then tear it away. Was very frequently used on women, whom it horribly mutilated.

**265 Smaller Iron Spider.**

**266 Mecklenburg Torture Stocks,** supported by a round strong iron stake, with hand and foot fasteners and padlock.

**267 Very Curious Iron Pillory;** place for the neck and for the hands was fastened with a padlock. The culprit was condemned to wear this terrible instrument so many days, weeks, or years. Early German.

**268 A Similar Iron Pillory,** somewhat lighter.

**269 Spanish Gaiter,** for torturing the foot, with strong screw and uneven tread.

**270 A Strong Iron Criminal Coupler or Whipping Stocks.**

**270a A Pair of Fine Steel Pincers,** for flaying or cutting away the skin, with inscription of Justice, &c.; also armourer's marks and ornamental design, &c.

**271 Executioner's Sword,** from Buchloe in Swabai, with exquisitely engraved blade. On one side is the motto:

> Wann ich das Schwert thu aufheben
> Wunche ich dem armen Sünder das ewige Leben.

Translation :—

> When I raise my sword, I wish the poor sinner eternity.

On the reverse :—

> Durch die Schärfe dieser Klingen
> Muss der Kopf vom Leib Wegspringen

Translation :

> From the sharpness of this blade the head must leave the body.

**272 Executioner's Sword,** from Ansbach, with twisted and gilt top; also pair of shears for cutting the hair on neck, and engraved with the following verses :—

> Die Herren steuren dem Unheil
> Ich exequire ihr End Urtheil.
> Wann ich das Schwert thu aufeben
> Wunche ich dem Sünder das ewige Leben.

Translation :—

> The world steers towards mischief and I execute judgment. When I lift up my sword God give the poor sinner eternity.

**273 Executioner's Sword** from Passau. On the blade is engraved :—Christ on the Cross, and under it, " Crucifixio Christi Et Verbum Caro.$=+Z+IA+BLZ+St+A+B+Z+H+GF+B$ factum." Under this is a medallion. On the reverse, Virgin and Child and the inscription, " Von Passau, Anno 1715." Underneath is $+Z+IA+$, &c.

**274 A Double Scold's Collar** for women, with pillories for heads and hands.

**275 A Scold's Collar** for one woman only.

**276 A similar Collar,** but of different shape.

**277 Hempen Whip,** with numerous barbed ends.

278 **Cat-o'-nine tails.**
279 **Long Chain,** with heavy iron shackle.
280 **Lighter Chain** for female offenders.
281 **Curious Wooden Mask or Brank** for horse stealers.
282 **Headsman's Sword,** leather hilt.
283 **Headsman's Sword** from Ingolstadt, with a pointed button, leather handle, a gallows and wheel damascened in copper on the blade.
284 **Headsman's Sword** from Amberg, with Iron grip, St. Michael and date 1726, and St. James. Under St. Michael there is Jesus Nazarenus Rex Judæorum, 1726, and under St. James an inscription.
285 **A Pair of Wrist-holders,** with padlock and key.
286 **Wire Flagellant,** with numerous thongs.
287 **Jointed Iron double Hand-fastener.**
288 & 289 **Gallows or Choking Rope.**
290 **Portion of the Flooring of a Prison.** Oak cut into diamond-shaped points, so as to be as hurtful to the prisoners as possible, and as in many cases the walls were also of the same material, it was very painful to lean, sit, lie, or stand.
291 **Iron Brank or Shame Mask,** with large ass's ears.
292 **Iron Mask,** with moustache. Highwaymen or freebooters were carried round the towns with this mask on, on various days before their execution.
293 **Whip** with which those who were exposed in the stocks were soundly thrashed in public according to sentence.
294 **Long Twisted Whip,** with heavier handle and thong, used on more hardened criminals, few of whom survived a sound application.

**295 Strong Rhinoceros Hide Whip.**
**296 Three-tailed Cat** (whip).
**297 Iron Braces and Body Ring,** with pair of manacles (see No. 298).
**298 Curious pair of Iron Braces,** with neck collar, handcuffs, and pair of shackles. This instrument fits over each shoulder round the waist, and when the victim is fastened by a collar round the neck, handcuffs, and shackles, he may be said to be a walking prison. He was literally bound in iron.
**299 Finger Pillory,** or flute-shaped instrument, which opens in a similar way to the collars, but this has ten partitions or divisions for the ten fingers; thus the offender stood in a public place exactly in the position as if playing the flute. Was used for various offences.
**300 Thieves' Wooden Lantern,** three-sided, and with movement to darken or show light at will.
**301 Branding Iron,** to brand culprit on shoulder or forehead.
**302 Branding Iron,** from Munich, brands the letter M.
**303 & 304 Two Branding Irons.**
**305 A Branding Iron,** brands E G O.
**306 Witches' Idol.** A small carved wooden figure of the devil, said to have been worshipped by witches.
**307 A small but formidable Pear-shaped Gag,** to prevent prisoners from screaming while under torture. (See No. 140.)
**308 Executioner's Sword,** from Augsburg, with shagreen handle and flat blade.
**309 Executioner's Sword** from Weissenburg, with verses. (See No. 272.)

*Catalogue of Instruments of Torture, etc.*

310 **Executioner's Sword** from Ansbach, with the following verse on the blade :—
>Die Herren steuren dem Unheil.
>Ich exequire ihr End Urtheil.
>J. N. R. J.

311 **Gallows Cord.**

312 **Turkish Bowstring, or Executioner's Cord.**

313 & 314 **Two Double Hand-fasteners.**

315 A very strong solid **Iron Double Manacle** at the end of strong iron bar.

316 **A ditto,** with long iron chain.

317 **Iron Mask,** with coat of arms and long speaking-tube in the place of a nose, worn by libellous persons and backbiters.

318 **Iron Polish Torture Stocks,** with two hand and two foot fastenings, double lock with keys, date 1472. When the prisoner was fixed in this, the position was most painful and unpleasant.

319 **Wooden Pillory for Hands and Long Chain.**

320 **Long Wooden Hand or Arm Breaker.** By pressure of powerful screws the hands or arm could be crushed completely.

321 **A Thieves' Wooden Lantern,** three sided and with movable slides.

322 **Spanish Boot,** made of two strong pieces of heavy wood, fitted inside with protruding iron knobs or buttons, and made to screw up so as to completely break the leg and inflict the most agonizing torture. (See engraving, No. 1033).

323 **Large Curious Prison Padlock and Key,** of extra strength.

C

**324 A Pair of Pincers,** for tearing out the tongue by the roots.

**325 A Cupping Machine,** which, when red hot, impressed the letter T.

**326 Very Curious Iron Brank,** with ass's ears and movable tongue and jaws, curiously embossed. The movable jaw denoted the scold or libeller.

**327 Iron Mask,** with ass's ears, small bells and protruding upper lip, worn for immorality.

**328 Large old Swedish Scold's Collar,** in the shape of a fiddle, with large bells and bell ropes, very curious.

**329 Strong Double Manacle,** with heavy iron bar and long chain.

**330 Venetian sharp Foot-presser,** of wrought iron, studded inside with spikes, which lacerated the flesh.

**331 Manacle,** with twelve-linked chain.

**332 Heavy Iron Whip,** with six sharp-edged iron lashes.

**333 Shackle,** with long iron chain.

**334 Curious very old Chain** for securing a prisoner by hands and feet.

**335 Iron Necklet,** with leather thongs and sharply-toothed ring for hanging or fastening the victim to a beam, or where he could just reach the floor on tip-toe.

**336 A Prison Warder's Weapon,** to be used on obstreperous or mutinous prisoners. It is in the shape of a whip, but the lash is of iron, with a weight at its end.

**337 to 340 Four various-sized Iron Shackles.**

**341 Iron Mask or Brank,** with female face, long horns, and donkey's ears.

Catalogue of Instruments of Torture, etc.    35

342 **Curious Shame Mask of Iron,** with long protruding beak and small moustache, also short ass's ears.
343 **Scold's Collar,** shape of the ruff worn by the women of the 16th and 17th centuries, but made of wood, hung round with 21 small bells and one larger one, and ornamented with a red and white tassel. In this the scold was led up and down the town or neighbourhood as a warning to her neighbours.
344 **A Pair of Strong Iron Martyr Tongs or Pincers** for tearing the flesh or for flaying.
345 **A Pair of ditto.**
346 & 347 **Heavy Wooden Hand Pillory,** bound in iron.
348 & 349 **Pair of Wooden Finger Squeezing Shears.**
350 **Judge's Staff,** an attribute of the presiding judge. The handle is handsomely ornamented.
351 **Long Iron Wire Punishment Rod.**
352 **Very Heavy Iron Double Foot Padlock.** With this fastened on, the prisoner could not possibly run away.
353 **A very similar Instrument.**
354 to 358 **Five Scolds' Wooden Collars** with apperture for head and both hands, slightly of different construction and periods.
359 **A Curious Yoke,** in which a couple found guilty of any act against the strict morals of the time were fastened and driven round the town, or stood in a market place. Early Swiss.
360 **A Long Iron Coupling Chain** with manacle at each end.
361 **Very Curious and Rare Pighead-shaped Wrought-iron Mask,** used with disgraceful offences.

The collection of branks or shame masks of various kinds and periods, many although but sparsely described here, will be found to be of the greatest interest to the student and the historian. The brank was very well known in England, and records of its use are kept in many Townships, and here and there in the Museums a specimen of it may be found.

**362 An Extra Large-sized Collar,** constructed for a male slanderer or libeller, who with head and both hands fixed in this uncomfortable appendage, was pilloried for a lengthened period in the market-place, an object of derision to all.

**336 Wooden Liar's Knife,** with burnt mark denoting a dragon. In the handle a whistle and bells with a set of printed verses pasted on, from the poems of Nuremberg's great writer, Hans Sachs.

Dass aufschneidt Messer
Wers kann machs besser.
*On the blade.*
Was soll ein Messer wanns nicht schneidt,
Oder steckt allzeit in der Scheidt?
Also was soll auch sein ein Mann,
Der nicht weitlich herschneiden kann.
*On the other side.*
Hettest du jezt fein still geschwign
So wär das Messer blieben lign,
Die Pfeiff ke in Schall het lassen hörn
Das Glöcklein teht sich dran nicht kehrn.

Translation same as No. 413.

Note.—This Knife is very curious as showing the style of treatment in those days of the drawers of the "long bow."

**364 Large Hand Axe or Heavy Knife,** used to chop off the fingers or hands of those found guilty of treason, killing a parent, and various other crimes.

*Catalogue of Instruments of Torture, etc.* 37

365 & 366 **Two Strong Hand-screws,** for squeezing the fingers.

367 **Chinese Executioner's Knife,** with engraved handle.

368 **Constable's Staff of Iron,** the end terminating in the figure of a man's fist. Could be used with serious results.

369 **Leather Body Ring,** with iron fastener. When the criminal was fastened with a ring round his body, shackles fastened from it to his feet, handcuffs to his hands, and a collar to his neck, he had little chance of escape or resistance. Slaves were frequently sold thus bound.

370 & 371 **Two Strong Iron Bars,** each with a manacle at each end, used for various purposes.

372 & 373 **Two very Curious and Powerful Thumb-screws.**

374 **Very Curious Iron Shame Mask or Brank,** with long straight protruding ears, long snout and overlapping lip (a sign of drunkenness), two curious round raised and blotched ornaments under each eye, and a deeply furrowed forehead. This was worn by confirmed topers, who were frequently condemned to stand exposed for perhaps a week, or longer according to the gravity of their failing.

375 **Another Iron Mask,** worn by thieves.

376 & 377 **Two Hempen Penitential Whips,** with strongly knotted lashes.

378 **Iron Body Belt,** with a manacle or handcuff fixed on to each side, and strong chain to fasten prisoner up to a wall or dungeon floor.

379 **A very powerful pair of Ankle Fasteners and Padlock combined.** With this on, the victim could not possibly walk a single step.

380 **Long Iron Chain,** with strong leg fastener at one end, padlock at the other.

381 & 382 **Two Strong Iron Shackles.**

383 **Curious Iron Brank or Shame Mask,** square face with turned up moustache and flattened nose, worn by people who were found to be very quarrelsome or combative.

384 to 388 **Five Wooden Scolds' Collars** of various sizes and designs, presumably from different towns.

389 & 390 **Two Gallows Choking Ropes.**

391 **Iron Body Ring with long Iron Chain.**

392 & 393 **A Pair of very Powerful Iron Finger-screws or Nail Breakers.** Inflicted most terrible pain.

394 **A very rare and uncommon Iron Brank,** made only in skeleton, but so constructed that parts cover the mouth, nose, and eyes, and with long outstanding head top. Was worn by a prisoner perhaps for years until his indentity was almost lost.

395, 395a, 396 & 396a **Four Long Iron Chains,** each with an ankle fastener at the end, worn in prisons while the inmates were at work, so that they could be fastened to their barrows, spades, or benches.

397 **A smaller Chain with Leg-holder and Padlock,** worn by a woman or child.

398 & 399 **A Pair of Double Thumbscrews,** with semi-circular tops and rings.

400 **A Witch's Idol.** A carving of the devil's head in wood, painted. This was worn by the supposed witch on her way to be burnt at the stake.

Burning to death was a very frequent punishment in all European countries; and in the olden time belief in witches was so strong that burning or drowning of some poor woman accused of "overlooking" or "bewitching" someone or something was nothing out of the common. On all such occasions a tablet such as shewn was worn on the way to doom.

401 **An extra strong Long Iron Chain**, with extra strong shackle at one end, and heavy padlock at the other, to secure some very determined culprit or evil-doer, most likely one who had been accused of slandering the reigning king or queen.

402 **Very Powerful Pair of Heavy Iron Leglets**, with arrangement to fit any size, and to lock on.

403 & 404 **A Pair of Iron Ankle Shackles.**

405 & 406 **A Pair of Double Thumbscrews**, to fasten up both thumbs; one with lock.

407 **A very Curiously Shaped Thumbscrew**, with extra powerful movement.

408 **A large Double Finger-screw**, so arranged as to close on two fingers of each hand. Very cruel.

409 & 410 **A Pair of Gallows Choking Ropes.**

411 **A strong Gallows Hook.**

412 **Sheath of an Executioner's Dagger.** Very early.

413 **Iron Liar's Knife**, with bells and rattles, engraved with the following verses on both sides of the blade and handle.

On the handle.

Das Aufschneidt Messr. Wers kan machs besser.
Hettest du jetzt fein still geschwigen
So wer das Messr ruhig blieben.—HANS SACHS.

TRANSLATION.—Who can do better for the Liar's Knife?
Had you quiet held your tongue
The knife still on the nail had hung.

On the blade.

Wann dein Maul redet was wer wahr,
Durften die Glöcklein nicht kommen dar
Und dich erinnern dass hinfort
Dich besinnst ehe du redst ein Wort.

TRANSLATION.—If your mouth speaks only true,
The bells they do not ring for you
To remind you that forsooth
You should only speak the truth.

On the other side.

Damit man nicht pfeiff oder leut
Dass jedermann merkt was es bedeut,
Dassdich dass Messer nicht verletz
Und dich in Spott und Hohn versetz.

TRANSLATION.—So that none may whistle or shout
And all know what this is about,
Let this knife bring you no shame
And nought but doubtful fame.

This knife was also used by people to show that they could not be imposed upon, the bearer being supposed to be himself "a sharp blade."

**414 Long Wooden Roller,** was used on the rack. The victim was stripped and then rolled over this uneven surface while being stretched until his bones were nearly all dislocated.

**415 A Fragment** of the cloak of the Christian Martyr Johannes Huss, who was burned at the stake at Constanz. See "Fox's Book of Martyrs."

**416 Iron Brank or Mask,** completely covering the face, with mouth in the act of whistling and with long ass's ears; worn by persons convicted of gluttony or other excesses.

**417 Half Iron Brank,** only covering the head, nose, and ears; very curious headpiece, in centre of which a candle was placed and lighted. Ordered by the Holy Inquisition. An exceedingly rare specimen.

## Catalogue of Instruments of Torture, etc.

**418 & 419 Two very Powerful and Painful Wrist Holders or Bracelets.**

**420 An Exceedingly Strong Iron Body Ring** with handcuff at each side and a 29-link iron chain.

**421 Very Curious Old Chain** with eccentric-shaped links and feet holders. The prisoner was fastened to a wall and left for days or weeks before being removed to confinement, so that all passers might see and remember the delinquent.

**422 Another,** somewhat similar, with strong padlock to lock on to leg.

**423 & 424 Two Shackles,** frequently used with the foregoing.

**425 & 426 Two Very Curious Early Prison Padlocks.**

**427 Iron Skeleton Mask,** from the town of Friedberg, near Augsburg, spectacled eyes, protruding nose, overlapping lip, and ass's ears. Worn by drunkards.

**428 & 429 Two Pairs of Leg Shackles,** each with strong iron chain. Worn during severe punishments.

**430 An Extra Strong Ankle Holder,** with long iron chain.

**431 A Similar,** lighter and smaller, for female prisoners.

**432 A Very Curious Wrought-iron Mouth Opener,** was placed between the teeth, which were then easily kept apart while the tongue was torn out, or boiling oil or molten lead was poured down the throat; also to force prisoners to eat.

**433 & 434 Two different Double Thumbscrews** for holding both thumbs.

**435 A strong double Hand-fastener of Wrought Iron,** with aperture to fix on end of chain. The victim was usually dragged along by a mounted police officer or at a cart's tail.

**436 Hair-Cord,** which, when put on and rubbed over the arms and feet, caused a most maddening irritation of the flesh.

**437 A Cloth Eye-binder,** with two raised parts, which pressed over the victim's eyes and kept them closed.

**438 A Choking Rope.**

**439 Crown of Straw and two Plaits.** This was worn by a fallen virgin. The victim was shorn of all her hair, and had to stand in a church door or other public place.

**440 Spanish Gaiter used for Torturing the Leg,** with very formidable uneven shin-bone presser.

**441 A somewhat similar one.**

**442 Another,** extra heavy and larger.

**443 Pair of Cruel Wood Pinching Shears** for breaking the fingers off after crushing the bone.

**444 An Iron Handscrew** for pressing the entire five fingers.

**445 Another,** somewhat different.

**446 to 449 Two Long Heavy Chains,** with heavy shackles for male prisoners, and two lighter and smaller for women or children.

**450 Iron Mask for Military Prisoners,** made in the shape of a helmet with long speaking-tube. Mouth and shield on forehead.

**451 Somewhat similar Iron Mask,** with flat face and protruding trumpet mouth. Shield on the forehead. Belonged to some feudal knight.

**452 Very Heavy and Massive Wrought-iron pair of Braces,** consisting of belt, two front bars, and shoulder irons, with strong padlock. When fastened up in this, all efforts at flight, resistance, or even rest, were of no avail.

453 **A very similar set of Irons.**
454 **Long Iron Stake,** with top cross-bar having an armlet at each end, long chain at bottom, with shackle for each foot. This in itself forms a complete imprisonment.
455 **Very heavy square linked Wrought-iron Chain and Foot Fastener.**
456 **Another similar, heavier.**
457 **Iron Head Crown,** with jagged nails inside. With this on, culprits were fastened to the wall.
458 **Terrible Spanish Spiked Iron Collar,** completely studded outside, inside, and on edges with sharp iron spikes so arranged that the wearer knew no rest, sleeping, waking, standing, sitting, or lying.
459 **Small Iron Wire Whip,** for flaying the victim while stretched on the rack.
460 **Torture Ladder,** about 15 feet long, with sharp three-cornered rungs, with cords and pulleys. On this a man was stretched to his fullest extent, to receive the torture which may have been ordered.
461 **Thief-catcher.** Very curious instrument, long iron handle, terminating at the top with a round hoop, garnished inside with triangular iron spikes. The front of the hoop is made to push open, so that the officer of the law can push it round the neck, arm, or leg of whoever he wants to catch, who on his or her part has no possible means of getting away, the ring having closed on him and preventing any effort to escape.
462 **Thief-catcher,** similar form.
463 **Wheel,** with strong protruding iron shaft so as to break the victim's joints.

**464 A curious Antique Iron Mask,** with long snout, for boastful people and liars.

**465 A long Chain and heavy Shackle.**

**466 A Curious Witches' Idol,** carving of a devil's head, supposed to have been worshipped by witches. See No. 400.

**467 A Mandragora Root,** cut into the form of a man, said to have great efficacy in the hands of witches against the person they were "overlooking." A nail or a needle driven into the mandragora caused a pain to shoot through the heart of the living man at the same moment, and nails or needles where driven into it until the person died. Also the mandragora was supposed to have the power of helping its owner to discover hidden treasure, &c., &c.

**468 A Long Chain,** with one very strong shackle at each end.

**469 & 470 A Pair of Ditto,** lighter.

**471 An old Hour-glass,** divided into hour, three-quarters, half, and quarter, by which the duration of the torture was timed.

**472 Strong Iron Body Ring, Pair of Iron Manacles.**

**473 Strong Iron Leg Ring, a Handcuff and Padlock,** attached to a long, strong iron chain.

**474 An Antique very large-bore Blunderbuss,** with wheel lock. Forbidden by International agreement.

**475 Large Wooden Brank or Shame Mask,** in the shape of a Death's head. This was worn by criminals who were pardoned the death penalty, and was worn by them in public places before being taken to the prison where they were incarcerated for ever.

*Catalogue of Instruments of Torture, etc.*

**476 A Thief-catcher,** similar to No. 461.

**477 Another Wheel,** somewhat similar to No. 463.

Breaking on the wheel was not a figure of speech, but a stern and terrible reality. When the condemned was laid out on the wooden bed and the wheel brought into action upon him and weighted with all the strength of the executioner and his assistants, every bone in the body was literally broken. In some countries the victim was tied on to a wheel and turned round and round as the waggon moved; he, sometimes over, sometimes under it. But here the combination of wheel and wooden bed seems much more cruel and lingering.

**478 Witch-catching Staff,** with the words, Jesus, Nazarenum, and Ave Maria. Under the iron point for prodding is also a hook for catching hold. This was so arranged that when a witch was to be caught it was unnecessary to touch her, as in those days of superstition no man could lay his hand upon a witch for fear of all sorts of evil spells. Catching hold of her with this staff, protected as it was by the words Jesus, Nazarenum, and Ave Maria, was considered to have the effect of circumventing all her machinations.

**479 Witch-catcher Staff** of a somewhat different kind.

**480 Curious Iron Mask,** with small eyes, with pointed beard and weathercock on crown, showing a changeable disposition or one given to untruths.

**481 Strong Iron Body Ring,** with two chains.

**482 Another,** lighter, with hinged movement.

**483 Curious Mask** without any face, with long speaking trumpet and snake on which to hang any stolen property; for thieves.

**484 An Iron Mask,** without face, long ass's ears for drunkards.

**485, 486, & 487 Three strong Iron Leglets,** with long chains.

**488 Large Iron Chandelier,** used for lighting the torture chamber.

**489 to 491 Three long Chains and Iron Fasteners,** various sizes and strengths.

**492 A Strong Circular Wood and Iron Pulley** and rope for running victim up to a beam, when his feet were heavily weighted until his joints were broken.

**493 Nobleman's very curious Iron Shame Mask,** shaped like a man's face, with movable visor and moustache, at each end of which is a bell; also one at each ear, a larger one at the point of the beard, and surmounted by two iron rods, each terminating in a bell. The use of this brank seems lost in obscurity, and we have searched in vain for its application; but there can be little doubt it was worn by malefactors of noble birth; and the idea seems to be that it was worn on the way to execution by a parricide, the bells being to call all the world's attention to the despicable criminal.

NOTE.—In England branks seem only to have been used for scolds; but in the cities of the Continent they were used for criminals of both sexes.

**494 An Executioner's Cord or Rope,** by which the delinquents were bound before going to execution.

**495 Another Executioner's Rope**, similar.

**496 to 554. A Large Collection** of strong iron manacles, shackles, and body rings of various times and nationalities.

> NOTE.—Although the space at our command will not allow us to individualize and describe each of these manacles, shackles, and chains, each and every one is different, made at different periods, and of various designs. They played a great part in the criminal history of Europe, having been used in every country. Criminals wore them in prison, in the torture chamber, at the stake, and in the Tumbril. In the penitent's cell they also found their place. In fact, volumes might be written on their use and abuse.

**555 A Model of the Guillotine**, made of wood, date 1793.

**556 A Metal Model** of same, differently constructed.

**557 Iron Coal Stove** on tripod feet. In this the coals were lighted and got to a white heat in order to make the branding irons red hot, and so burn the marks or letters into the flesh of the forehead or back.

**558 Iron Coal Box** for same purpose.

**559 Pair of Bellows**, used for blowing up the fire in above. The history of branding is so well known that it is needless to enter into it here. Both men and women were branded in all European countries for all sorts of crimes, and even in the earlier times a serf bore his master's brand mark.

**560 The Condemned's Cup or Mug.** Made of glass, with engraving of the crucifixion. Out of this cup the condemned was given wine to drink during his last day.

**561 An Antique Fayence Beer Jug**, with burnt-in picture of Hiesel and his big dog.

**562 Punishment Officers' Drum.** This small, long, four-cornered, iron-bound oak drum or rattle was used to call all wayfarers, and passers' attention to the culprit, so that all might see, hear, and take warning by the punishment thus being meted out.

**563 Soup Bowl and Spoon.** This was used to affix to a scold's collar, in which two females were fastened, so that if, as it frequently happened, the shame of the punishment did not bring the combatant females to a renewal of friendship and forgiveness, they were reduced by *hunger*. The bowl was hung close under their noses, filled with soup or stew; the women had one hand loosened, and were glad to eat out of the same bowl, using the only spoon one after the other. This was taken as a sign of returning affection.

**564 Iron Wristscrew,** of great cruelty, with outward roughed movement for lacerating the arm.

**565 Spanish Gaiter** for torturing the leg, with strong screw and roughed inner movement for crushing the shin bone.

**566 Ditto,** with similar movement, different screws.

**567 Another,** of different construction.

**568 Another,** different.

**569 Another,** different.

**570 Another,** larger and more powerful.

**571 Another,** with an addition of sharp iron teeth in base.

**572 Another,** still different, with double screws for entirely crushing the leg bone.

**573, 574 & 575 Three very curious and different large Prison-gate Padlocks.**

## Catalogue of Instruments of Torture, etc.

576 & 577 **Two Scolds' Wooden Collars**, with aperture for neck and both hands.

578 **A large Wooden Winder or Pulley**, used to stretch criminals.

579 **Ditto**, of wood and iron.

580 **A long Wooden Spiked Hare**, with strong spikes. (See No. 89.)

581 **Strong Iron Neck Collar**, with outstanding iron rod with bell on end, so that prisoner could never move without giving warning.

582 **A Witches' Idol Figure of the Evil One**, which witches were supposed to worship.

583 **An Iron Chandelier**, somewhat similar to No. 488.

584 **Curious barred face Helmet or Mask**, worn by juvenile criminals.

585 **A Poacher's Flint Gun** made of iron, formed so that it looks like a mountaineer's stick, with a chamois horn handle, the lock made so that it can be taken off and put on at will.

586 **Prison Whip**, with thorn handle.

587 **An Extra Heavy Brank, or Punishment Hat, for Lazy People.** It is of Iron, and with iron bars across the face.

588 **Instrument used to draw knots of cords as tightly as possible.**

590 **Pentitent's Cap made of Linen**, with opening for eyes, ears, mouth, and nose.

591 **Executioner's Staff**, carried before the execution. Wooden handle, with red and white rings.

592 **A Set of Stocks with Place for two Culprits.** In these delinquents of almost all kinds were placed, for varying periods, exposed to public gaze and scorn.

**593 Penitent's Linen Shirt.**

**594 Executioner's Cloak,** very long, of red woollen material, presumably red so as not to show blood spots or stains.

**595 Wonderful Wooden Chain** of many links, with hanging spoons. This work of patience was done by Baron von der Trenk whilst in prison, and cut out of a plank of wood, with no other tools than the knife he was allowed to cut his bread with. What makes this chain the more remarkable is that it has no joints of any kind, is neither nailed, screwed, or glued, but is entirely self-containing, and cut out of the solid. Baron von der Trenk was imprisoned for high treason at Magdeburg about the year 1754; released 1763.

**596 A Heavy Stone,** used for stretching.

**597 Another,** similar weight.

**598 A Pair of Stone Bullet Weights.**

**599 An Iron Ball Weight.**

**600 A Heavy Pair of Weights.**

**601 A Heavy Stone Weight.**

602          Ditto.

603          Ditto.

**604 Spanish Mantle, or Drunkard's Cloak and Helmet.** This so-called cloak is really in the form of a long barrel, wider at the bottom than at the top. It was hinged at the back so as to open. The drunkard or ne'er-do-well was placed in it, and it was closed to and locked, the top having an iron-bound orifice just large enough to let his head through. On his head was placed the barrel helmet, through which he could see and be seen by all. The period of confinement was varied according to the offence or its frequency. One or two hours was the usual sentence. To tall men this was more severe than to short ones. Whereas a tall one, standing up, would lift the entire wooden barrel on his shoulders, and would after a time, borne down by its weight, have to sink on to his knees, a short man would be able to stand inside and so suffer far less pain.

"Several historians, dealing with the social life of England in bygone times, have described the wearing of the barrel after the manner of a cloak as a general mode of punishing drunkards in force during the Commonwealth. Mr. Ralph Gardner, of Cheriton, in the County of Norfolk, printed in 1655 a work, in which he says, 'He the deponent further affirms that he hath seen men drove up and down the streets with a great tub or barrel, opened in the sides, with a hole in one end to put their heads through, and so cover their shoulders and bodies down to the small of their legs, and then close the same—called the new-fashioned cloak, and so make them march to the view of all beholders; and this is their punishment for drunkards and the like.'

"It is noticed in *Travels in Holland*, by Sir William Brereton, under the date of May 29th, 1634, as seen at Delft. John Evelyn visited Delft on August 17th, 1641, and writes, 'that in the Senate House hangs a weighty vessel of wood, not unlike a butter churn, which the adventurous woman that hath two husbands at one time is to wear on her shoulders, her head peeping out of the top only, and so led about the town as a penance for her incontinence.' Samuel Pepys has an entry in his diary respecting seeing a similar barrel at the Hague in the year 1660. We have traces of this mode of punishment in Germany. John Howard, in his work entitled *The State Prisons in England and Wales*, 1784, thus writes, 'In Denmark some criminals of the lower sort, as watchmen, coachmen, &c., are punished by being led through the city in what is called 'The Spanish Mantle. . . .' I measured one at Berlin. This mode of punishment is particularly dreaded, and is one cause that night robberies are never heard of in Copenhagen."—*Old Time Punishments*, W. ANDREWS.

From the above it appears that not only was it used for drunkards, but also for burglars, bigamous women, &c., &c.

**605 A similar Spanish Mantle or Drunkard's Cloak** without Helmet, from Munich.

**606 A somewhat similar one** from Lauingen in Suabia.

**607 Weighty Stone** in the shape of a coat-of-arms shield, and dated 1661. This somewhat great weight was hung by a chain round the neck of the accused. Crimes such as theft, assaults, &c.

**608 A similar Stone** used for field or garden thieves. It is engraved with a head, and has on the top a crown of flowers and some fruit.

**609 A similar Stone** for gamblers, with deeply-cut engravings of playing cards.

**610 Very large-sized Double Brank or Shame Mask,** shaped like the fiend's head, with horns, protruding eyes, and teeth. Belonging to this are also a snake and dragon's head. This hideous mask was worn by a women who had daily assaulted her husband. As in all these old punishments, the culprit stood in a most public place. In this instance the snake or dragon was held in the hand. It signified that the holder was a house dragon, and as such, deserving the scorn and obloquy of all beholders.

**611 Wooden Tablet** with the word mörder (murderer) written on it. This was worn by a criminal convicted of murder. On it was also inscribed a written notice of the executioner's as to particulars of the crime, date of execution, &c.

**612 Large Wooden Stocks,** in which a condemned culprit was forced to lie tied up in a market or public place so many hours daily, fastened by the feet, and with a tablet bearing his name, description of crime, and punishment. In most cases he was also sentenced to receive so many whippings per day or week, which were applied by the public executioner.

## Catalogue of Instruments of Torture, etc.

613 **Iron Chair.** Was frequently used as a ducking-stool to duck scolds or supposed witches.

614 **Tablet worn by the Occupant of Stocks.** This one was evidently worn by fruit or field thieves.

615 **Baker's Ducking Cage.** Very curious oak cage, about six feet high. Inside is a seat. In this cage the baker who gave short weight was locked up, and the cage was then hung to chains and drawn up and down in the water until the occupant was nearly drowned. See engraving, No. 709.
NOTE.—This ducking cage was not known in England. There are many ducking stools still extant, but from all inquiries we find that they were only used to duck scolds or women charged with witchcraft.

616 **Large Oil Painting,** by Michael Angelo di Caravaggio, showing *Man's First Crime*, Cain killing his brother Abel.

617 **Seat or Settle belonging to a Torture Chamber,** with one half for the physician and the other for the executioner. It will be noticed that the part intended for the doctor has a back to lean against, whilst the executioner's part has not.

618 **Small Table** on which there is a sharp-toothed thumb and finger screw, an instrument which the victim must have seen with a shuddering sense of fear, so ingenious is it in its cruelty.

619 **A Pair of Heavy Weights.**

620 **Torture Chair,** covered on the seat with wooden spikes, so that the occupant could not sit without being severely punished, the more so as his feet were often weighted with heavy stones to add to his pain.

**621 The Spiked Portion of a Torture Seat.**

**622 Torture Chair,** the back, the seat stretcher, foot-rest, completely covered with sharp wooden spikes, so that the occupant was tortured sitting, leaning, standing; in fact after a short time the pain became unbearable.

**623 Heavy wooden Torture Seat,** with front lockable iron bar so that the victim could be securely fastened in. In this chair tortures of all kinds were inflicted.

**624 Torture Rack,** about 10 feet long, with "spiked hare," round roller, and all the necessary cords for binding and stretching the victim.

**625 Torture Cradle,** about 5 feet long, completely covered with wooden spikes, and with wooden spiked movable cushion (?) head rest.

**626 Stretching Gallows,** known in German as Schlimme Liesel (Fearful Eliza). At the foot are strong iron rings, into which the man's feet were placed; his hands were then fastened to a triangle, which was raised by means of ropes and pulleys until he was stretched beyond endurance. When in this position he was perhaps flayed, or else cruelly whipped at stated periods by the public executioner.

**627 Spanish Donkey.** This terrible instrument is formed with a $\wedge$ or cone-shaped top, worked to a sharp point. The victim was placed straddle-legged on this, and heavy weights placed on each foot, until the sharp point of the donkey's back cut clean through his body, or broke him right in halves.

**628 Whipping Bench,** from Berlin. A large bench upholstered, straps to fasten the arms, legs, head, and feet, with a movable footboard, to be raised according to the height of the whipper.

629 **Ball** for prisoner's leg.

630 **The Wooden Bed** on which the victim of the wheel was laid.

631 **Heavy Iron Execution Chair.**

The culprit sat or kneeled in the chair, with head leaning over the back, and the headsman, after cutting away the hair, with one stroke severed the head from the body.

632 **A large heavy Bell,** which was rung all the way the condemned was being taken to the block or scaffold. Backwards and forwards, forwards and backwards, swung the bell, until the executioner was ready to do his gruesome work.

633 **The Mummified Head of a Beheaded Nuremberg Child Murderess,** together with the spear on which it was shown at the wheel.

635 **A Pair of Bronze Candlesticks** which were chained to the altar, same period.

636 **The Celebrated Original IRON MAIDEN (Eiserne Jungfrau).** This terror-inspiring torture instrument is made of strong wood, coated with iron. Opens with two doors, to allow the prisoner to be placed inside. The entire interior is fitted with long sharp iron spikes, so that, when the doors are pressed to, these sharp prongs force their way into various portions of the victim's body. Two entered his eyes, others pierced his chest, and, in fact, *impaled* him alive in such a manner that he died in the most agonizing torture. Persons were condemned to death by the embraces of the *Iron Maiden* for plots against the governing powers, parricide, **religious**

unbelief, and murder with attempt against puberty. The date of this rare specimen is the fifteenth century.

It is believed that the iron maiden is purely and peculiarly a relic of old Nuremberg, as at that date we do not read of it anywhere else, whilst the annals of that town contain many allusions to its terrors.

We find that in the next (16th) century there was an instrument of execution in Scotland known as the "Maiden," but it was perfectly different to this one, and was really a beheading block on to which a knife fell from a certain height, and something after the style of the present guillotine—a much more merciful and expeditious mode of execution than the slow, cruel, lingering death above mentioned. As we said in our preface, the fiendish ingenuity displayed in inventing terrible torture is in no instance more in evidence than in the construction of this relic of ancient Nuremberg, known as "The Iron Maiden."

**637 An Engraving** showing the "Iron Maiden."

**638 An Old Painting** on panel, "Justice," with the inscription :—

"Gott ist grecht in sainn Gericht drum thu gutts und sündge nicht."

Translation :—

"God's judgment is aright; do thou good, and sin not."

This was fixed over the Judge's seat.

**639 Small Panel Painting.** "The Sign of the Ban of Blood," showing an axe and a severed hand.

**640 A similar Panel.**

*Catalogue of Instruments of Torture, etc.*

641 **Stone Tablet**, which hung over the entrance door to the torture chamber, with the inscription :—
"Atris patratis sunt atra theatra parata."
Translation :—
"Dark deeds make dark endings."

642 **A Papal Bull**, dated Rome, 5th February, 1492. Written in Latin on parchment, giving an authority to the Abbot of St. Aegidus, in Nuremberg, to hold and constitute Courts of Justice in that town.

643 **A Witch's Charm** of lead, with engraved characters and motto.

644 **Wooden Model of the Witch's Castle**, near Straubing, in Lower Bavaria ; here the notorious Agnes Bernauer was accused of being a witch, and as such kept until she was drowned in the Danube.

645 **Oil Painting of the Gilder, Erdmann of Nuremberg.** He was the last man publicly tortured in Nuremberg. After his death he was found to have been innocent of the crime of theft to which he had *confessed* under torture, and in consequence of this lamentable miscarriage of justice it was decided that torture should be for ever abolished in the town.

646 **Picture of the Guillotine** on wood.

647 **A Curious 15th Century Forerunner of the Mitrailleuse or Gatling Gun**, constructed so as to fire fifteen balls at one time ; was in those days called a *Hell Machine*, and its use was forbidden by the International agreement as being outside the pale of fair warfare.

648 **Thumb Instrument, or Press**, with two pressers for thumbs.

**649 A Set of Stocks with Wheels,** so that they could be wheeled about to any part of the City or from Town.

**650 A Wooden Windlass** for running the victim up to the ceiling, where he was suspended by the thumb, with weights attached to his feet.

**651 Portrait of Maria Renata of Wurzburg,** who was the last woman burnt at the stake in Germany for being suspected of witchcraft, 21st January, 1749.

**652 Oil Painting of a Bavarian Court Jester** who was bricked in alive, with his hands tied behind him, at the Castle of Trausnitz, and so left miserably to starve to death.

*Catalogue of Instruments of Torture, etc.* 59

# The Collection of Prints and Engravings,
## SHOWING THE APPLICATION OF THE VARIOUS TORTURES IN DIFFERENT COUNTRIES.

**700** Descriptive account of the capture of the Bavarian robber, Hiesel.
**701** Tumult at Middleburg, in Holland.
**702** Man on stretcher being singed to death.
**703** Print showing the application of manacles, shackles, &c.
**704** Portrait of Judica Widman, wife of the executioner of Nuremberg, 1672.
**705** Louis XVI. brought back from Varennes to Paris, June 25, 1791.
**706** "La malheureuse famille Calas."
**707** Dick Turpin and Black Bess.
**708** The execution of the two famous castle thieves at Berlin, 8th June, 1718.
**709** The Debtors' Bridge at Nuremberg, showing debtors' towers for males and females, and also a baker being dipped for fraudulent weights.
**710** Picture showing a person being branded on back, forehead, and cheeks.
**711** Execution at the Hague, 1619.
**712** Torture and execution of women.
**713** Three terrible modes of execution.

714 Portrait of a Swiss rebel, beheaded near Lucerne in 1653.
715 Prisoner chained, and with iron collar.
716 Portrait of Suess Oppenheimer, the fraudulent Finance Minister of Wurttenburg.
717 The same, executed in a cage.
718 Wife of Widman, the Nuremberg executioner.
719 Execution of Counts Struensee and Brand, Copenhagen, 1772, and their crests being destroyed by the headsman.
720 Arrest of a notorious thief.
721 Portrait of Simon Fraser, Lord Lovat.
722 Picture of a prisoner in chains.
723 A decapitated head exposed on the wheel.
724 Execution of two thieves at Hamburg.
725 Massacre in the Low Countries.
726 Scene during the French Revolution.
727 Episodes during the life of Jack Rann.
728 The robber Hiesel, his son and dog (coloured).
729 Portrait of Beatrice de Cenci, after Guido Reni.
730 Sixteen portraits of notorious criminals.
731 Portrait of Lieutenant Schiedel, who captured Hiesel.
732 The Fortress of Hohenstein, where Oppenheimer was imprisoned.
733 Execution in the Low Countries, 1584.
734 Execution of Councillor Gosson at Atrecht (Arras) for not joining the rebels, 20th October, 1578.
735 Strangulation of the Grand Vizier Cara Mustapha by order of the Sultan, February, 1684.
736 Portrait of Philip Egalité.
737 Man being publicly whipped on the stocks.

## Catalogue of Instruments of Torture, etc. 61

738 Madame Elizabeth, sister of Louis XVI.
739 Portrait of Johaun Beuckels, Provost of Munster called Jan Van Leyden.
740 Capture of Louis XVI. at Varennes, 22nd June, 1791
741 Jan Smit hung by his foot at Haarlem, in 1572.
742 Suess Oppenheimer in prison, and his trial.
743 Execution of Andreas Hofer, the Tyrolean patriot, outside the walls of Mantua.
744 Portrait of Robespierre.
745 Portrait of P. Schaeffer.
746 Portrait of Anckerström, murderer of the King of Sweden.
747 Portrait of Wilhelm von Grumpach, 1567.
748 Death of Gustav the Fearless, King of Sweden, at a ball, by the hand of an assassin, 16th March, 1792.
749 Portrait of the Count Cagliostro.
750 Portrait of the Emperor Joseph II., during whose reign torture was relinquished in Germany.
751 A prisoner suffering the bastinado.
752 The man in the iron mask.
753 Engraving of a female cheat in Strasburg.
754 Showing Algerius, student of Padua, burned at Rome in 1557.
755 Execution of Louis XVI.
756 Execution of the regicides, Counts Struensee and Brand at Copenhagen, 28th April, 1772.
757 Massacre by the Spaniards in the Low Countries.
758 Damien tortured and being torn to pieces by four horses; his remains burnt.
759 Terrible massacre at Haarlem after the capture of the town by the Spaniards, 13th July, 1573.

760 Portrait of Wiedman, the Nuremberg executioner.
761 Henri Masers de Latude, incarcerated during thirty-five years in different State prisons.
762 Portrait of Carl Sand, murderer of Kotzebue.
763 A military execution.
764 Engraving showing a man having his eyes burned out.
765 Execution of Marie Antionette on the Place de la Revolution, 16th October, 1793. Her last words were, " Farewell my children ; I go to rejoin your father."
766 Massacre in the Low Countries by the Spaniards.
767 The memorable address of Louis XVI. at the Bar of the National Convention, 26th Dec., 1792.
768 Plan and Elevation of the Bastille.
769 A prisoner being led to execution.
770 A murderess in prison, in chains.
771 Thomas Muncer, preacher, executed at Alstet, Thuringia.
772 The robber Hiesel, his son and dog.
773 Calas taking leave of his family.
774 Bohemian rebel.
775 Attempted murder of Henri Quatre, by Ravaillac, during a public procession.
776 Portrait of Jacob Clements, the murderer of Henry III., King of France, 1st Aug., 1589.
777 Execution of eighteen noblemen at Brussels, June 1st, 1568, by order of the Spaniards.
778 Four people condemned to be burnt by the Inquisition.
779 Portrait of Kaspar Hauser.
780 Execution of a general for having given his town over to the enemy.

*Catalogue of Instruments of Torture, etc.* 63

781 Portrait of Johann de Witt.
782 An execution in the interior of a prison.
783 Terrible torture of a woman at Maestricht.
784 Terrible torture inflicted at Veer in Zeland in 1560.
785 Attempt to kill Napoleon I. with an infernal machine, 25th December, 1800.
786 The son of Louis XVI. being shown the guillotine.
787 Execution of French delinquents for having attempted the life of Prince of Saxony at Cologne, 13th June, 1704.
788 Dulcinus and his wife torn limb from limb at Novara, 1308.
789 The guillotine.
790 Arrest of the rebel, Johann David Miller.
791 Robert Dudley, Earl of Leicester, Baron of Denbigh, Governor of the Low Countries.
792 Portrait of the murderer of P. Forster in prison.
793 Count Cajetani tried and executed for alchemistry.
794 Statue of the Duke of Alba.
795 Execution of Louis XVI.
796 Five views showing the trial, deposition, imprisonment, taking the Sacrament, and lying in state of Charles I. of England.
797 Execution at Buchloe, Bavaria, 1777.
798 Drowning and hanging rebels at Bonn, on the Rhine.
799 Execution of Counts Egmont and Van Horn, June, 5, 1568, at Brussels.
800 Cecilie Renaud arrested at Robespierre's house in 1794.
801 Portrait of Suess Oppenheimer.
802 Hiesel's attempt to escape from prison.

803 Engraving showing twenty-four criminals, some handcuffed, some with shackles, some with jougs.
804 Allegorical picture, "The Angel Delivering Man from Satan's Influence."
805 A culprit being exposed in a cage.
806 Cruelties by the Spaniards in the Netherlands.
807 A female fortune-teller paraded through the streets of Nuremburg in 1801.
808 The Duke de Nemours in Prison.
809 The Duke of Orleans, Philip Egalité.
810 Drowning of French subjects in the Loire by order of Carrier, 1793.
811 The Duke of Alba treacherously summonses Counts Van Horn and Egmont, and has them seized.
812 Rebels being led to execution.
813 Portraits of three Frankfort rebels.
814 Lucretia Grenville, who attempted Cromwell's life.
815 The wounded Robespierre being carried into the vestry-room of the Committee of Public Safety.
816 Execution of rebels in front of Town Hall at Leipzic.
817 A famous robber and his gang being taken to prison.
818 The Spanish auto-da-fé.
819 Hungarian preachers sent to the galleys in 1674.
820 Attempt on the life of Joseph I., King of Portugal, and execution of the plotters, in 1759.
821 Execution in London, subject unknown.
822 Various modes of execution.
823 Showing various executions.
824 Ann Hendricks, burned at Amsterdam, 1571.
825 A public execution.
826 Scenes in the life of a noted criminal.
827 Twelve portraits of notorious criminals

## Catalogue of Instruments of Torture, etc. 65

828 Prisoners at work.
829 Assassination of Prince of Orange, 15th March, 1582.
830 The death of Kotzebue.
831 Portrait of Wilhelm von Grumpach.
832 Attack on the village of Jonckersdorff, near Cologne, 3rd July, 1556.
833 Execution at Frankfort, 1616.
834 Public execution of a woman at Ansbach.
835 Print showing Suess Oppenheimer in cage (coloured).
836 Kaspar Hauser's grave at Ansbach, with poem.
837 Execution of six persons, Vohlan, in 1661.
838 The brothers de Witt, executed and mutilated.
839 Pouring boiling oil down prisoners' throats at Poitou, in 1685.
840 Louis XVI. and his family.
841 Arrest of the famous robber, Schinder Hannes, and his band.
842 Episodes of the murder of the Mayor of Liège by Count Varfuse.
843 Portraits of plotters against William of Orange of England, and history of the plot.
844 Execution of Cajetani at Custrin in Pomerania, 1709.
845 Engraving showing the execution of the Duke of Monmouth on Tower Hill, July, 1685; and in same frame the execution of the Marchioness of Brinvilliers.
846 Scenes during the Rebellion at Mastricht, 1576.
847 Portrait of Kohler, who was executed for blasphemy.
848 Portrait of Frederick van der Trenck.
849 Coloured engraving showing the landing of Murat, King of Naples, at Pizzo, 8th October, 1815.

E

850 Portrait of Stortzenbecher, Hamburg pirate, who was executed.
851 Execution of the robber Hiesel.
852 The brothers Bigedini, tortured and afterwards executed at Mantua for high treason.
853 Revolution at Vincennes, 28th February, 1791.
854 Cruelties inflicted by President Massaut at Niort, in 1664.
855 Portrait of the Countess Valois de la Motte.
856 Execution in Brabant, 1570.
857 Suess Oppenheimer being escorted to the place of execution.
858 A meeting of the French revolutionary party in Paris, 1793.
859 Portrait of Roesner, and his execution.
860 Burning and Torture of Jews in Vienna, 1642.
861 Showing a prisoner in chains.
862 Louis XVI. being led to execution, accompanied by his Confessor, Edgeworth.
863 Engraving showing various vices and their resulting punishments. In this print will be seen many of the instruments of torture as described in this Catalogue.
864 Human sacrifice in the East.
865 Execution of Louis XVI., 21st Jan., 1793, whose last words were, " I die innocent of the crimes of which I am accused. I never wished anything beyond the happiness of my people, and my dying prayer is that Heaven may forgive them my death."
866 J. B. Ziermann, a notorious murderer, executed at Rudolstadt, May 29, 1767.
867 Jean, a merchant at Cordova, led about with his face turned to an ass's tail, and then burned in 850.

## Catalogue of Instruments of Torture, etc. 67

868 The drowning of Marie de Monjou, 1552.
869 Trial and execution of Roessner at Thorn, in Prussia.
870 Camille Desmoulins preaching revolution, July 12, 1789.
871 Excesses by the Spaniards in the Low Countries.
872 Execution at Prague in 1621.
873 Man confronted by a murderer.
874 Episodes in the life of Hiesel.
875 Engraving showing prisoners secured in various ways in a prison cell.
876 Execution of Edward Digby, Thomas Winter, and others, in London, 1606.
877 Arnoldus, reader at Brixen, burned as a heretic at Rome, 1145.
878 Birds'-eye view of the Chateau de Vincennes, where the Prince de Conti and others were arrested.
879 Hiesel being conducted to the court-house.
880 Interior of the State prison in Venice.
881 Charles VI. orders the dishonourer of his wife to be sewn up in a sack and thrown into the river.
882 Execution of the Gunpowder Plot Criminals in London.
883 Suess Oppenheimer in a cage surrounded by spectators.
884 Portrait of John George Wogaz, a notorious thief, who stole in October, 1788, valuable pictures from the Dresden Gallery.
885 Plan of the old torture prison in Nuremberg.
886 Execution of Sand at Mannheim, 1820.
887 Execution and torture at Berlin, 8th June, 1718.
888 Massacre and torture of the Huguenots.
889 An Englishman, John Brett, burnt at Antwerp, after having had his tongue torn out, 1576.

**68**     *Catalogue of Instruments of Torture, etc.*

**890** Massacre in Ireland about 1644.
**891** Terrible torture at Antwerp, 1576.
**892** Robber being broken by the wheel.
**893** Engraving showing a man being stoned to death.
**894** George Wanger, beheaded at Brixen, 1591.
**895** The whipping of a woman.
**896** Portrait of Suess Oppenheimer and his mistress.
**897** Portrait of Beatrice de Cenci, with inscription.
**898** Murder at Stettin, scene of the murder, and culprit in prison.
**899** Portrait of Cartouche, his imprisonment and execution.
**900** A letter from the Vehmgericht, dated 1509, with seal and coat-of-arms, inviting Heyntz Kone to come before the judgment, addressed thus:—

"Ane Heyntz Kone komme diesse Brieff Dissen brieff sol niemandt vffthun lessen odder horen lessen er sy dan eyn echt recht freyscheffe des heimlich freyen Gerichts."

("This letter is for Heyntz Kone; no one must open it, hear it, or read it, but this is a real free letter of the secret free judgment.")

**901** Engraving showing the use of the antique blunderbuss, (see torture instruments).
**902** Portrait of Widman, the headsman of Nuremberg.
**903** Execution of rebels at Frankfort, 1616.
**904** Execution at Prague, June, 1621.
**905** Engraving showing a man being roasted to death.
**906** Parricide having his hands cut off, and another executed.
**907** Sacking of a Dutch town, and torture of the inhabitants.
**908** A notorious robber and his boy being examined before the Judge.
**909** Murder of General Wallenstein, Duke of Friedland, at Eger, 1634.

## Catalogue of Instruments of Torture, etc.

**910** Coloured print of Hiesel and his boy and dog.
**911** Public exposure of a murderer outside the Town Hall at Nuremberg.
**912** Attack on the Prince of Orange at Delft, 10th July, 1584.
**913** Persecution of the Protestant Ministers in Hungary, 1674.
**914** A woman being buried alive at Brussels, 1597.
**915** Portrait of Damien, "the greatest monster on earth," murderer of Henri Quatre.
**916** An engraving, showing man being flogged.
**917** Murder of a Burgomaster.
**918** Imprisonment and execution of Brothers Rennebaum.
**919** Episodes in the life of Hiesel.
**920** Female accused of arson, in prison.
**921** Portrait of Widman, Nuremberg executioner, born 1675.
**922** James Bolland, executed for forgery.
**923** Murder of Marat by Charlotte Corday, 13th July, 1793.
**924** Portraits of Mme. de Brinvilliers and another.
**925** Louis XIV. taking leave of his family.
**926** View of the State prison in Venice.
**927** Portrait of the head of a gipsy band who was executed on the wheel in 1733.
**928** Execution of Gray and Baxter at Whitehall.
**929** Schinder Hannes, his wife and child.
**930** Beginning of the French Revolution, first emeute in Faubourg St. Antoine, 28th April, 1789.
**931** A celebrated robber discovered hiding in a beer-barrel.
**932** Burning of the town of Ulm by the French, with map of the district.

## Catalogue of Instruments of Torture, etc.

**933** Portrait of the French General Melac, who devastated Germany.
**934** Jesuit Conspirators against the King of Portugal.
**935** Tortures inflicted on the Swiss by applying red-hot irons to their hands in 1214.
**936** Execution of a woman in London, subject unknown.
**937** Executions at the Hague.
**938** Heinrich Emkens being burned to death with lighted straw at Utrecht in 1562.
**939** Criminals being whipped and otherwise tortured, previous to being burned to death, at Bruges.
**940** Burning of criminals at Ghent, 1578.
**941** Portrait and execution of Count of Tattenbach, executed at Gratz, in Styria, 1st December, 1671.
**942** The fortress of Hohenstein prison, of Wurttemberg.
**943** Public exposure of a perjurer at Augsburg.
**944** The son of Louis XVI. executed before the eyes of his father.
**945** Portraits of five female criminals.
**946** Portrait of Karl Ludwig Sand.
**947** Prisoner in chains.
**948** The Bavarian Robber, Toni, in Prison, 1786.
**949** Damien chained to his iron bed on which he was carried to the judgment-chamber, and on which he could be tortured without being released.
**950** Portrait of Jan van Leyden.
**951** Portrait of a notorious malefactor.
**952** John Grosch, handcuffed in prison.
**953** Geleyn Cornelius hung by his thumb, with weights to his feet, afterwards burnt, 1572.
**954** Henry II., of England, doing penance at Thomas-a-Beckett's grave.

## Catalogue of Instruments of Torture, etc.

**955** Engraving showing an execution guillotine in Rome.
**956** Punishments in the 18th century.
**957** A notorious criminal being exhibited in a cage.
**958** View of the dungeon where the torture instruments were exhibited at the Royal Castle of Nuremberg.
**959** Capture of Hiesel and his dog.
**960** Scene at a public execution.
**961** Capture of Hiesel.
**962** Engraving showing Sand in prison.
**963** Death of General Dillon at Lille, 29th April, 1792.
**964** Execution of a general at Innsbrück.
**965** Hiesel at a country inn.
**966** Murder at an inn at Nuremberg.
**967** Execution of two thieves outside the palace at Berlin.
**968** Public exposure of a perjurer previous to his being guillotined.
**969** Portrait of Mary Lafarge.
**970** Engraving showing a man stretched perpendicularly, and being flayed alive.
**971** Showing a man being stretched on stretching bench preparatory to flogging.
**972** Interior of a prison, and various punishments.
**973** A prisoner being visited by monks.
**974** An exposure on the wheel.
**975** Three martyrs sewn in sacks and drowned at Aix-la-Chapelle, 1560.
**976** The arrest of a woman by an officer of police.
**977** Execution of De Previl at Arras.
**978** A group of martyrs being burned at Salzburg, 1528.
**979** Execution of about 350 persons near Mayence, by order of the Crown, and various modes of death, 1529.

980 Origines tortured at Alexandria in the year 254.
981 Fearful cruelties perpetrated in the Netherlands by the Duke of Alba, 1567.
982 Sacking of a town and massacre of the inhabitants.
983 Executions in Hungary.
984 Portrait of a murderer at Munich.
985 Runck, the dishonest keeper of the royal castle at Berlin.
986 Portrait of John Christopher Neumann, thief and son of thievish parents.
987 Female convicted of arson, in chains.
988 Death of Robespierre.
989 Portrait of the famous robber, Schinder Hannes.
990 The prisoner of Chillon.
991 Engraving of a medal of Charles I. of England.
992 Portrait of Thomas More.
993 Simon, guardian of the Bastile.
994 Portrait of Count Struensee, murderer of the King of Denmark.
995 Portrait of William, Earl of Kilmarnock, beheaded in London, 29th August, 1746.
996 Peasants measuring a matrimonial yoke.
997 Titus Oates in the Pillory.
998 Portrait of Christian Müller, of Stolpe.
999 Portrait of Egmont.
1000 Portrait of Sir Walter Raleigh, beheaded in London, 19th October, 1618.
1001 Print showing the application of the iron Joug. The Joug of St. Goar on the Rhine.
1002 Portrait of Mary Queen of Scots.
1003 The Temple, the celebrated prison of Louis XVI.

## Catalogue of Instruments of Torture, etc.

**1004** Portrait of Kaspar Müller, called "Gallows Kaspar."
**1005** Berend Knipperdolling, Provost of Münster, in Westphalia.
**1006** Prisoner chained with belt, handcuffs, &c.
**1007** Thomas Howard, Duke of Norfolk.
**1008** The Bridge of Sighs, at Venice.
**1009** Erdman, who was innocently tortured in Nuremberg.
**1010** Portrait of Thomas, Count Amalfi, the Neapolitan rebel.
**1011** Portrait of the son and successor of the Nuremberg executioner, Widman.
**1012** Portrait of Kaspar Hauser.
**1013** Portrait of Eppelein von Gailingen, the famous bandit who jumped on horseback from the walls of the Castle of Nuremberg.
**1014** Scene at a public execution.
**1015** Showing male and female prisoners at work, each one wearing a neck or head-iron with bell (see No. 23).
**1016** Curious old print showing various modes of torture, men being flogged, flayed, hanged, burned, broken on the wheel, &c., &c., and with following motto: "Scopus Legis est aut ut eu que punit emendet, aut poena eius caeteros melliores reddet aut sublatis malis caeteri securiores vivat."
**1017** Engraving showing metal bull with Christian martyrs inside being roasted to death; also shewing tortures of water and weight.
**1018** Perspective showing the buildings of the Schwabach prison and torture-house, with man receiving the bastinado.

**1019** Regulus the Roman General being headed into a barrel with spiked nails, preparatory to being rolled down a hill by the Carthaginians.

**1020** Engraving showing the execution of a famous robber band, some being hanged, broken by the wheel, and the chief being decapitated.

NOTE.—The following twenty-nine engravings are taken from the celebrated Torture Law-book, "Constitutio Criminalis Theresiana," which book contains the series of laws passed by the Empress Maria Theresa of Austria, &c., &c., and dated Vienna, the last day of December, 1768. It appears that up to this date torture could be inflicted at the will and decree of any governor of a province, judge, or feudal lord. The Empress, however, determined that laws should be passed not only limiting these powers, but minutely detailing the various crimes for which torture was to be allowed, the mode and form in which it was to be applied, and giving drawings, diagrams, and descriptions of the instruments to be used, as follows:—

**1021** The thumbscrew, its application and directions for use.

**1022** Diagram showing formation of the thumbscrew.

**1023** Showing how the thumbs should be placed when applying the thumbscrew.

**1024** Showing prisoners under the torture of the thumbscrew.

**1025** The punishment of the cord, showing the formation and appearance of the binding-cord.

*Catalogue of Instruments of Torture, etc.*

**1026** Showing the application of the cord, with diagram of the human arm under the infliction of the torture of the binding cord.

**1027** The arms bound together with the cord.

**1028** Showing the stretching ladder, with details as to binding the prisoner preparatory to being stretched.

**1029** Prisoner bound on stretching ladder, with winding apparatus for stretching him.

**1030** Another diagram of the stretching ladder, with prisoner being stretched.

**1031** Showing the formation of the bundle of candles used for burning portions of the condemned's body while on the stretching ladder.

**1032** Prisoner undergoing the torture of burning while on the stretching ladder.

**1033** Three engravings showing the formation of the Spanish boot (see No. 322), with diagrams giving mode of application.

**1034** Prisoner undergoing the torture of the Spanish boot.

**1035** Four engravings showing the thumb-presser, its formation and application.

**1036** Three illustrations giving details of bench or seat on which victim was laid or sat preparatory to being bound, with diagram showing the hands fastened together.

**1037** Four illustrations showing wheel and hoist with which the condemned was raised, giving also particulars of weights which were to be attached to his feet, and diagram of man being so run up.

**1037**A Three illustrations of the spiked shinbone pressers, their formation and use.

**1037**B Portrait of King Charles the First.

**1037**C Portrait of Lady Jane Grey.

**1037**D Portrait of Krauss.

# The Collection of Engravings and Prints,

## SHOWING THE OLD TOWN OF NUREMBERG, ITS SURROUNDINGS, CUSTOMS, AND COSTUMES.

**1038** Public shooting competition in Nuremberg, in 1614, and procession attending it.

**1039** Church of the bare-footed monks as it was before the fire in 1671.

**1040** Soldiers entering the old town.

**1041** The former fortress of Lichtenau, near Nuremberg.

**1042** The square near the Neuenthor, Nuremberg.

**1043** View of the Castle Grunsberg, near Nuremberg.

**1044** View looking towards the hospital gate at Nuremberg.

**1045** Festival of cross-bowmen at Nuremberg.

**1046** View of the Frauenthor at Nuremberg.

**1047** Front view of the Nuremberg Arsenal.

**1048** The house of the ancient family of Von Grundherr in 1356.

**1049** View of the five-cornered tower of the castle of Nuremberg.

**1050** Encampment of the Franconian troops outside Nurember in 1793.

**1051** View of Nuremberg Castle, on ascending the hill.

**1052** Encampment of French troops near Nuremberg in 1796.

**1053** Nuremberg beadle in old costume.
**1054** The Frauenthor at Nuremberg.
**1055** View of the Imperial Castle at Nuremberg.
**1056** Armoured Knight on horseback, 16th century.
**1057** Pencil drawing of the Rosenau at Nuremberg.
**1058** View of the Castle.
**1059** View of same from another aspect.
**1060** View of the Town from the Worterthor.
**1061** Views of the St. Egidus Church and School in 1696.
**1062** View of the Town after the burning of the above Church, 1696.
**1063** Nuremberger Militiamen in 1803.
**1064** The Church of Our Lady at Nuremberg.
**1065** Burning of Ulm in 1688.
**1066** Jollification of peasantry at a fair.
**1067** Public games at Nuremberg, fencing, &c., &c.
**1068** Carthusian Chapel.
**1069** St. Walburgi's Church.
**1070** The gate of the Castle.
**1071** View of Nuremberg and poetic description of same.
**1072** View of Gostenhof suburb of Nuremberg.
**1073** The Cemetery of St. John near Nuremberg.
**1074** View in the Büchenglingen wood near Nuremberg, and public entertainments therein.
**1075** The hotel of the Golden Goose, formerly the house-of-call of the royal mails, date 1701.
**1076** A member of the legal profession in olden times.
**1077** The Cloister Church in Nuremberg.
**1078** Conrad Fürleger, governor of the town fortress in 1679.
**1079** Portrait of Nicolas Muffel, senator, born, 1410, died 1469.

1080 View of the Pfalzgrafenstube at Nuremberg.
1081 View of Town and Castle.
1082 The annual festivities of the Guild of Fishermen.
1083 Undertakers of the olden times.
1084 Castle Hiltpoltstein near Nuremberg.
1085 View of the Castle from the cemetery.
1086 Fire at the Church of St. Egidus.
1087 Panoramic view of a procession of soldiers marching from the Arsenal to the Castle.
1088 A series of eight coloured prints showing the following ceremonies:—1. Procession of foundlings on St. John's Day. 2. Annual Christmas fair. 3. Carol Singers. 4. Councillors inspecting the bread. 5. Examination of the children in the churches. 6. Proclamation of the Easter fair. 7. Ceremony of proclaiming the freedom of the city. 8. The drummers beating in the New Year.
1089 The Church of St. Leonard, 1612.
1090 View from the old Town Hall, 1614.
1091 The prison at Bamberg, where witches were incarcerated.
1092 Plan showing the position of the Swedish troops before Nuremberg in 1632.
1093 Festivities of the Butchers' Guild.
1094 View of the hospital gate.
1095 Explosion of the Nuremberg powder mill, 1766.
1096 The grand hall of the Rathhaus.
1097 The inner courtyard of the Castle of Nuremberg showing Queen Cunnigunde's lime tree.
1098 A set of four costume engravings.
1099 View of the fortifications of the Town.

1100 Three hawkers of the olden time.
1101 Panoramic view of the Town, 1599.
1102 The Castle of Rotheberg, three miles from Nuremberg, date 1703.
1103 The Emperor Charles' Chapel at Fuerth, near Nuremberg, built in 838.
1104 The Mayor, attended by Councillors, going to the Town Hall.
1105 Coloured view of the Castle towards the west.
1106 The White Tower, 1701.
1107 Ascent of the æronaut Blanchart on the 16th November, 1787. Coloured print.
1108 Picture showing condemned wine, seized and taken towards the river by the authorities.
1109 Winter festival, sledge drive given by the Mayor of Nuremberg in honour of Count Stolberg in 1763.
1110 The band of the militia in early times.
1111 Procession of the German Emperor Leopold, attended by the patricians of the Town, 1658.
1112 A Nuremberg patrician and attendant going to the Council in 1620.
1113 View from the wooden bridge over the Pegnitz.
1114 Parade of the Royal Bavarian National Guard at Nuremberg in 1812.
1115 The Landauer Chapel, 1700.
1116 View of St. Jobst in 1702.
1117 View over the Pegnitz, the debtor's bridge.
1118 The fruit market.
1119 Four engravings of costumes.
1120 Annual meeting of the crack shots.
1121 St. Moritz Chapel, with funeral procession.
1122 View of St. Jobst, near Nuremberg.

*Catalogue of Instruments of Torture, etc.* 81

1123 A bridegroom and bride of the nobility.
1124 Very old view of Nuremberg Castle.
1125 View of the Haller Gate, with two bridges over the Pegnitz in 1693.
1126 The Franciscan Church in 1126.
1127 The meat market in Nuremberg in 1680.
1128 View from the Castle.
1129 View from the bridges.
1130 Personifications of various Nuremberg slang terms.
1131     Ditto              ditto
1132 View of an overflow of the river.
1133 Ruins of the Emperor Charles' Chapel at Fuerth.
1134 Coloured print showing eight different grades of inhabitants of Nuremberg.
1135 The town-crier and his attendants.
1136 The Hallerthor at Nuremberg, from the exterior.
1137 Pencil-sketch view of Town.
1138 The sentinel on the ramparts.
1139 Another view of the old lime-tree at Nuremberg.
1140 The Church of St. John.
1141 Procession and entry of the Emperor Joseph in 1704.
1142 View of Nuremberg near the park gate.
1143 The water-gate at Nuremberg.
1144 The hostelry of the Red Horse in 1701.
1145 View of the Sophia spring at Grünsberg.
1146 Foundations of old buildings.
1147 Procession of the Guild of Clothworkers in 1722.
1148 Entry of the German Emperor, Matthias I., 1612.
1149 View of the Castle towards the town.
1150 Winter diversions near Nuremberg.
1151 Nuremberg female peasant, 1701.
1152 Lady of Nuremberg, with rain cloth, 1701.

F

1153 A Nuremberg lady walking, 1701.
1154 Great banquet in Town Hall at Nuremberg to celebrate the peace of 1749.
1155 Plan showing town and neighbourhood.
1156 Guild procession in 1687.
1157 The entrance gate at St. Peter.
1158 A Town Councillor.
1159 A merchant.
1160 Attendant at funerals.
1161 A bridegroom of the Patrician order.
1162 A battle near Nuremberg in 1657.
1163 Nuremberg star singers.
1164 Drummers.
1165 A Patrician bride.
1166 A jester.
1167 Characteristic impersonations of Nuremberg terms.
1168 A bird's-eye view of Nuremberg, 15th century.
1169 Distribution of presents from the windows of the Town Hall.
1170 View of the Park.
1171 The fortress of Nuremberg looking west.
1172 View from the Lauferthor.
1173 The corn market.
1174 Competition of cross-bow men in 1768.
1175 View outside the Nuremberg Town Hall on the occasion of paying homage to Charles VI., on the 18th January, 1712.
1176 View of Nuremberg, with key to buildings, &c.
1177 Curious building at Nuremberg in 1646.
1178 Twelve ancient costume pictures in one frame, with poetic inscriptions.
1179 Four large coloured views of the different gates of Nuremberg.

Catalogue of Instruments of Torture, etc. 83

1180 Post at St. Rochus.
1181 View of Nuremberg Castle.
1182 An inviter to a wedding and a toast-master.
1183 Four female costumes.
1184 A peasant and his family on the way to church.
1185 View of the Town Hall from St. Sebald.
1186 Inundations at Nuremberg; 1784; water-colour drawing by Prasch.
1187 The chimney sweeps' of Nuremberg annual outing.
1188 Plan of a fortification of Nuremberg.
1189 Twenty characteristic engravings of Nuremberg slang terms.
1190 View of Charles' Chapel with four saints.
1191 Procession of the old Guilds, the Tapemakers and Bellfounders.
1192 Overflow of the Pegnitz in February, 1784.
1193 View of the Laufergasse in Nuremberg.
1194 Three clergymen in ancient costumes.
1195 A Nuremberg peasant.
1196 View from the Castle.
1197 View from the river island at Nuremberg.
1198 View of the Castle Courtyard.
1199 Procession of the Guild of the Turners on the 21st September, 1700.
1200 Twenty-four characteristic skits of Nuremberg.
1201 Perspective view of the Rathhaus with burgomaster and councillors.
1202 A Nuremberg market woman.
1203 Four processions of the Guilds of Compass-makers in 1688.
1204 A Jewess going to the Synagogue.
1205 A Nuremberg clergyman.

84 *Catalogue of Instruments of Torture, etc.*

**1206** A Jew going to the Synagogue.
**1207** A view of Stein near Nuremberg.
**1208** The annual lottery in the Rathhaus.
**1209** View from the Lauferthor.
**1210** Very curious work done by Johann Leonard Tauber at Nuremberg in 1752, being a representation of a ball and cross, all composed of the six degrees of the Christian faith, Luther's catechism with explanation, the morning and evening prayers, and great many other portions of Holy Writ, all written with pen and ink. In the rose alone is the Lord's Prayer entire. This can all be distinctly read with a magnifying glass.
**1211** Two coloured engravings. The bridegroom and two pages, the bride and two town councillors.
**1212** The Poet's wood near Nuremberg.
**1213** The five-cornered tower.
**1214** Two views of St. Moritz Chapel, one as in 1300 and one as in 1313.
**1215** Pencil drawing of General Tilly, commander of Imperial troops at Nuremberg, 1634.
**1216** The gymnasium with gymnastic performances.
**1217** The St. Margaret's Chapel in the Castle.
**1218** Procession of Sausage-makers, an antique usage in early times, 1658.
**1219** The Observatory, at Nuremberg, 1716.
**1220** The Engelthal Convent near Nuremberg.
**1221** The famous lime-tree.
**1222** The fort of Reicheneck near Nuremberg.
**1223** Water colour showing the Thiergaertnerthor.
**1224** Ditto, the Lauferthor.
**1225** Ditto, the Hospitalthor.

## Catalogue of Instruments of Torture, etc. 85

1226  Water colour, the Neuerthor.
1227  Ditto, the Wördterthor.
1228  Ditto, the Frauenthor.
1229  View of a square in Nuremberg.
1230  A similar view.
1231  Lawelshof, a suburb of Nuremberg.
1232  A coloured plan of the encampment of Swedish troops before Nuremberg, 1632.
1233  A dedication on the 100th jubilee of the cross-bowmen in 1782.
1234  View of Town Hall, 1671.
1235  A miracle outside the five-cornered tower in 1631.
1236  Burning of the Church of St. Laurence.
1237  View of Betzenstein, near Nuremberg.
1237A  A Nuremberg mouse trap dealer.
1238  The burg from the east side.
1239  Coloured prints, outside suburbs of Nuremberg
1240  The Cemetery of St. Rochius.
1241  The Haymarket in Nuremberg, 1701
1242  A town singer.
1243  Entrance to a pleasure-garden in the park.
1244  View of a pleasure-garden.
1245  The St. Augustin Convent.
1246  Plan of the floods showing height of waters in 1595 and 1784.
1247  St. Martha Church.
1248  Inspection of the bakeries by the Commission.
1249  The fishermen's competition on the river.
1250  The junior burgomaster on his way to town.
1251  The summoning officer and his attendants.
1252  Three judicial officials.
1253  Two Nuremberg girls in costume, with poetic description.

**1254** A guild's procession.
**1255** View of the Spittlerthor and Arsenal.
**1256** Large view of Nuremberg with key, after Lorenz Strauch.
**1257** Battle between French and Austrians outside Nuremberg in 1800.
**1258** Murder of two young Viscounts of Nuremberg.
**1259** The Twelve Carthusian brothers.
**1260** Street scene in Nuremberg.
**1261** Old view.
**1262** Costumes of the 17th Century.
**1263** Pencil drawing of one of the gates.
**1264** The great market and beautiful fountain.
**1265** Road leading to the castle.
**1266** Funeral of a Nuremberg Patrician, 1794.
**1267** A wedding at home amongst the nobility.
**1268** The five-cornered tower.
**1269** A similar view.
**1270** Departure of the French in 1801.
**1271** View from the Lauferthor looking towards the Wöertherthor.
**1272** View near the Neuethor.
**1273** View on the frozen river, with skating.
**1274** View of the large bronze fountain, by George Schweigger, in 1660.
**1275** Exhibition of relics at Easter.
**1276** View of the Town in 1511.
**1277** Chase of a thief or beggar.
**1278** Siewel tower of Nuremberg.
**1279** View of the burg.
**1280** A Nuremberg toast-master.
**1281** The Fleischbrücke.

1282 St. Nicholas Chapel.
1283 The fruit-market in 1725.
1284 The Castle, looking north.
1285 Street in Nuremberg towards the Spittlerthor.
1286 Pen-and-ink drawing, view of the town.
1287 Large view, with key.
1288 Hostelry or house of call for merchants from Leipzig fair, and where the Customs' examination took place.
1289 The Fleischbrücke, looking towards the Castle.
1290 A view of the Castle.
1291 Counting-house of the firm of Bestelmayer.
1292 Nuremberg councillors going to church after the election of Emperor Leopold II., as Romish Emperor of Germany, 1790.
1293 The Nuremberg Patricians.
1294 The wheat brewery.
1295 A milk-seller.
1296 St. Walburgi's Church.
1297 Isle of Nuremberg and riding school.
1298 View on a lake near Nuremberg.
1299 Two foundling children.
1300 The Judenbüler postern.
1301 View after the battle between Austrians and French, outside Nuremberg in 1800.
1302 The town jester.
1303 Interior of the Armoury, 1728.
1304 Fishing on the Dutzenteich.
1305 A female going on sentry duty.
1306 The fencing school.
1307 The sport of bull fighting, 1795.
1308 Imperial troops before Nuremberg, 1785.

1309 Old house near the castle.
1310 The French troops leaving Nuremberg in 1796.
1311 View of the Lauferthor.
1312 Large interior of St. Lorenz Church, 1696.
1313 Large interior of St. Sebaldus Church, 1693.
1314 Burning of a watermill.
1315 Interior of the opera house.
1316 The island of the Pegnitz.
1317 Fisherman's hut near the lake.
1318 The Pellerhaus.
1319 Public gardens.
1320 Coloured print of the five-cornered tower of the Castle of Nuremberg.
1321 Large wooden coat-of-arms which hung outside the gate of the Castle of Nuremberg while the town was under the dominion of Austria.
1322 Cherry-stone, on which are minutely and exquisitely carved 113 eminently characteristic heads of emperors, princes, popes, and other historical persons. Highly interesting and unique specimen, the masterpiece of the celebrated Nuremberg carver, PETER FLOETNER, who lived there in the early part of the sixteenth century. It is specially mentioned in JOHANN NEUDORFFER's book on Nuremberg artists, and was formerly in the collection of Art Treasures at Bayreuth Castle, the ancient seat of the Margraves of Brandenburg.
1323 Oil painting. View of Nuremberg.
1324 Oil painting. View near Nuremberg. Winter scene.
1325 Oil painting. Map of Nuremberg, period of the thirty years' war.

See Catalogue No. 1016.

See Catalogue. No. 071.

See Catalogue, No. 905.

See Catalogue, No. 970.

See Catalogue No. 882.

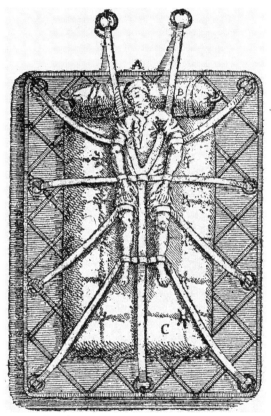

See Catalogue, No. 949.

See Catalogue No. 953.

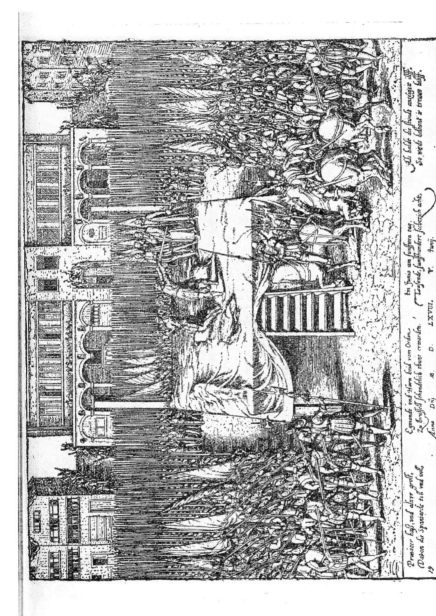

See Catalogue, No. 709.

See Catalogue, No. 1017.

See Catalogue, No. 1019.

See Catalogue No. 939.

See Catalogue No. 1020.

# J. ICHENHÄUSER

## ART EXPERT,

### Dealer in Rarities, Antiquities, and Curiosities

---

**ANTIQUE FURNITURE, TAPESTRIES, ARMS, ARMOUR,
VALUABLE CHINA, BRONZES, GEMS,**

AND

## Paintings by the Old Masters

---

### WOOD CARVING AND SCULPTURE
OF THE MOST ARTISTIC DESCRIPTION.

---

### Speciality for the Restoration of
China, Paintings, Tapestries, and Furniture

---

*VALUATIONS FOR PROBATE AND EXPERT OPINIONS.*

---

### DESCRIPTIVE CATALOGUES PREPARED
For Collections of anything pertaining to Art.

---

MR. ICHENHÄUSER may be consulted personally, or by letter, at his address,

## 68, NEW BOND ST., LONDON, W.

LESSEE AND RESPONSIBLE MANAGER—

# LEE BAPTY, F.R.G.S., &c.

*To whom all communications regarding the Collection should be addressed.*

CENTRAL OFFICES—

## QUEEN VICTORIA STREET, LONDON, E.C.

"LEE BAPTY, LONDON."

# HISTORY OF CHIROPODY

## BY

## FELIX VON OEFELE M D

*New York N Y*

[This monograph originally appeared as Chapter I in the text Book of Chiropody edited by Dr M J Lewi and published by the School of Chiropody of N Y]

[1914]

## INDEX

| | PAGE |
|---|---|
| FOREWORD | 3 |
| THE FOOT IN THE HISTORY OF PRIMITIVE MANKIND | 5 |
| THE WORDS FOR FOOT | 7 |
| THE WORDS FOR TOE | 10 |
| THE WORDS FOR NAIL | 12 |
| THE WORDS FOR FOOTWEAR | 15 |
| THE FOOT IN ZOOLOGY AND IN COMPARATIVE ANATOMY | 16 |
| THE ABORIGINAL HISTORY OF PODIATRY | 20 |
| THE GENERAL HISTORY OF SHOES | 22 |
| THE HISTORY OF BEAK SHOES | 31 |
| THE PREDECESSORS OF MODERN FOOTWEAR | 37 |
| DENOMINATION OF HELOMA | 39 |
| HISTORY OF THE PRACTITIONER OF CHIROPODY | 48 |
| SUPERSTITIONS OF THE OLD TIME CHIROPODISTS | 53 |
| HISTORY OF THE SURGICAL AND MEDICAL TREATMENT OF CORNS | 58 |

# CHAPTER I
# HISTORY OF CHIROPODY

### BY

## FELIX VON OEFELE M D

*New York N Y*

# INDEX

## OF

## CHAPTER I

| | PAGE |
|---|---|
| Foreword | 3 |
| The Foot in the History of Primitive Mankind | 5 |
| The Words for Foot | 7 |
| The Words for Toe | 10 |
| The Words for Nail | 12 |
| The Words for Footwear | 15 |
| The Foot in Zoology and in Comparative Anatomy | 16 |
| The Aboriginal History of Podiatry | 20 |
| The General History of Shoes | 22 |
| The History of Beak Shoes | 31 |
| The Predecessors of Modern Footwear | 37 |
| Denomination of Heloma | 39 |
| History of the Practitioner of Chiropody | 48 |
| Superstitions of the Old Time Chiropodists | 53 |
| History of the Surgical and Medical Treatment of Corns | 58 |

CHAPTER I

# HISTORY OF CHIROPODY

## FELIX VON OEFELE M D

## FOREWORD

CHIROPODY, in its primitive sense comprehends that branch of minor Surgery which has to do with the treatment of helomata, or corns, by the use of the knife. A later discussion of the origin of the term heloma will indicate the possibility of the term chiropody being entirely expunged so that the practice of foot lesions may hereafter be styled "Helotomy" or, "Heliatry," or more generally "Podiatry." Corn-cutting has, through all the ages, been considered a very minor form of surgery—so insignificant, in fact, as to have been entirely eliminated from the practice of the physician and the surgeon. There has never been any education accorded the student chiropodist other than that which he acquired from watching his preceptor at work on the foot of a patient.

All science, particularly that of medicine, is divided and subdivided into specialties; however, no set of medical men ever undertook to specialize in diseases of the foot and its appendages and so it has happened that this kind of work took on the character of a trade and was carried on by those who were not scientifically equipped for their work. The layman was, of course, ignorant of the limits of chiropody—he simply knew that his doctor did not treat cases of cosmetic foot troubles and accordingly he turned to the so-called chiropodist for assistance for his foot-woes with the thought that he was securing the fullest measure of assistance obtainable by those afflicted as he was.

The primitive notions as to chiropody continued until the chiropodists themselves, self-educated and self-inspired, realized that their calling was entitled to scientific supervision and development. They have organized a School to educate their successors and the compilation of this Text Book is the first real step in the literature of Chiropody along scientific lines. They have come to the conclusion that the chiropodist should know all of the relations as to cause and effect as they obtain to abnormal foot conditions. This in turn comprehends the need for their being well educated in the study of Anatomy, Physiology, Histology, Materia medica, Therapeutics, Bacteriology, Pathology, Surgery and Foot Gear.

Inasmuch as the law at present limits the scope of the work of the chiropodist to the cosmetic treatment of the feet, the practitioner of this branch of medicine must be able to recognize diseases and conditions which require the care of the practicing physician and surgeon and for this purpose his education should also include a knowledge of Chemistry and of Hygiene. The patient in the chiropodist's chair may manifest symptoms of arthritis urica or syphilis or nephritis or consumption or of other local manifestations of a systematic disease. The chiropodist should be so educated as to be able to recognize these and thus to intelligently direct the patient to the care of the practicing physician.

The chiropodist should be able to speak understandingly with the physician. It is not to be expected that every chiropodist shall have a pedantic knowledge of Greek and of Latin, but he should be familiar with the scientific terms of all conditions and diseases to which his attention may be directed in the pursuit of his professional work. The chiropodist should also know the history of his calling just as an individual strives to be familiar with his genealogy. If we do not know ourselves how can others be expected to acquire full knowledge of us?

The present Text Book cannot contain all that is necessary for this purpose, but in it is made the attempt to prepare the necessary foundation for augmented knowledge along all of these lines. So that a close study of all that is contained within this volume will equip the practicing chiropodist in a manner never before attempted. It is sure to be useful.

## THE FOOT IN THE HISTORY OF PRIMITIVE MANKIND

Primitive mankind knew the foot and its uses. They studied it comparatively as well as subjectively and were wont to compare the human pedals not only with the feet of animal creation, but also with the underpinning of objects such as chairs and tables. In the south of France there are evidences in caves, of the development of writing in characters from the first drawings of objects such as human beings. The feet were drawn in profile. These drawings developed into picture-writing and then into hieroglyphics representing complete words, then syllables, then single letters. It is not entirely improbable that the modern lower case "b" of the European alphabets is but a modified picture of the foot below the knee as the letter "o" is a modified picture of the eye. Besides the aboriginal pictures of some American Indian tribes we are aware of three systems of writing by pictures common among peoples of the old World.

The Eastern-Asiatic picture writing was introduced in China about 2000 B. C. These hieroglyphics have been changed so that today they are indiscernible. They represent only spoken words as we know them today, in groups of pictures which are not clear.

A second kind of characters were used many thousand years B. C. among the peoples inhabiting the valley of the Euphrates and the Tigris. Oriental diplomacy found use for them throughout western Asia and evidences are not wanting to show that they were contained in letters to Egypt and other foreign countries. The boundaries of the East were, however, probably not limited to this group of hieroglyphics. They are found chiseled in stones from periods of time most-remote. They were usually depicted by the use of only straight drawn lines. In this way the drawing of the disc of the sun became a square. Later on these characters were outlined in clay tablets. The beginning of every line was thick and heavy. They are today classified as the Babylonian cuneiform inscriptions and are still better known in the more regular Assyrian style. They were also used for the oldest Persian alphabet.

The Egyptians used a third or special kind of hieroglyphics. The original drawings were inscribed on the walls of buildings.

The ancient Egyptian hieratic style, on paper, is less discernible than the wall inscriptions. The latest demotic style reproduces the original pictures as little discernible as the cuneiform inscriptions. Parts of the foot, the entire foot and feet in different positions are very common in these inscriptions.

⾜ is the Chinese sign of the human foot and is pronounced *kiŏ*. Its equivalent is 足. The foot of the bird is indicated by a special sign similar to the cuneiform word for foot.

The cuneiform inscription for the foot is ⟨☰; for both feet it is ⟨☰⟩⟩ with the figure "2" as a suffix. The Englishman, the German and the Russian all pronounce "2" as "two" in their respective languages. The Sumerian designates this cuneiform picture of foot as *nir* and the Accadian Semit uses *shepu* for the same. The Assyrian sign is as given above. The true Babylonian inscription for the foot is ⟨≥.

The Egyptian hieroglyphics designated the foot or feet in various positions. The inscriptions on the walls run both from left to right and from right to left, but the faces of the various hieroglyphics always present themselves towards the reader. From the foot to the knee represents the sign for the sound of the letter "*b*." ⌋ and ⌊ are frequently found in keeping with the above statement. The usual writing however, is from right to left and is always found thus on papyrus paper. The hieratic shortened shape is ⌊.

Our modern letters have a long history. They passed from nation to nation, from country to country and were modified again and again through the various centuries of their use. Many of our modern letters are derived from hieroglyphics. We cannot trace the history of the modern lower case *b* farther than to the people of Etruria. The Etrurian shape of the letter *b*, more than two thousand years ago, was similar to the above hieratic letter of the same sound. It is barely possible that this letter *b* was intended as a modified picture of the foot. More than 6000 years ago, in the prehistoric language preceding the old Egyptian kingdom, the foot was probably called *ba* or some other word creating a similar sound.

In addition to the phonetic expression by letters, the hieroglyphics contain ideographic signs. There the conception of foot was drawn ⌋. It was also possible for very short writing that ⌋ indicated right foot, and that ⌊ indicated left foot. From left to right ⋏ means to approach and ⋏ to recede; if from right to left, the converse is the correct reading. The feet were also combined with other signs in the hieroglyphic inscriptions. ᛚ represents a little crock. In such vessels the ancient Egyptians kept their ointments. Many of these ointments, as we will learn, were cosmetic substances for the nails of the hands and feet. But 𓂻, representing the above little crock with two approaching feet is the hieroglyphic expression for convey or conduct or carry.

We cannot go deeper into the details of hieroglyphic writing; those interested should consult special books on the subject.

From 3000 to 2000 B. C. it was difficult to express in language the emphatic *me* or *you*. The part or organ, supposedly active was specifically mentioned. "I myself go" was then expressed "my foot goes." The foot occurred in many other phrases. It would lead us too far if we attempted to collect and here present proofs of the importance of the foot in old and new languages as evidence of preferable phraseology and more elegant expressions. Such expressions were ofttimes characteristic. The medieval Latin through all of Europe said "a capite ad calcem" as expressing the whole human body; it means "from the head to the heel." The Chinese have a like expression, but they start from the feet, which is suggestive of their natural submissiveness; they say "from the feet to the head."

Arm and foot were also used by primitive mankind as a standard of measure. Later on a legal average foot became necessary. The French revolution more than 100 years ago abolished this primitive standard. Progressive nations followed, the only exceptions being England and the United States of America, both of which still use the aboriginal "foot" for the purpose.

### THE WORDS FOR FOOT

English and most other languages spoken in the United States of America, derive their origin from Europe. Most of these belong to the Aryan family of languages. In very remote times there was only one language, which in turn produced the later languages, as children and grandchildren. This original old Aryan language designated the foot as *pad*—with some suffixes. From this root the expressions for foot in the other languages originated, as for instance, old Indian or Sanskrit *pâdas* "the foot." In the Lithuanian language the word *pâdas* is still preserved, but means only the sole of the foot. In the ancient Grecian language *pûs* is the foot and *pódes* the feet; in the Greek

Aeolian dialect, *pôs* is the foot; in Latin *pes* is the foot, *pedes* the feet.

In the north of Europe the family of German languages is derived from the old Aryan language. But many letters have been changed by a rule of sound displacement. The *p* changes regularly to *f* and the *d* to *t*. The old Gothian word *fôtus* is in this way the same as the Sanskrit *pâdas* and means the same. The *s* also changes very often, but not regularly, to *r*. The old Icelandic language has the word *fôtr*. Most of the other later languages dispensed with the suffixes. The foot is called in old English and in old Saxonian *fôt;* in Swedish *fot;* in Danish and Norwegian *fod;* and in Dutch *voet;* in real English *foot*.

In the special German languages the *t* is changed to *z* and to *ss*. The foot is called in old High German *fuoz*, in middle High German *vuoz* and in modern High German *fuss*.

The Slavonic languages are another group of the Aryan languages of eastern Europe. The derivatives of Sanskrit *pâdas* are there lost in the meaning of foot. The Russian calls the foot *noga* and the Polonian styles it *nog*. We will again meet with these words when explaining the words for nails of the toes.

The English language is a branch of the family of Germanic languages; but about half the words of the English language are derivatives of the Latin language. The children of the Latin language are the Romanic languages. The French language calls the foot *le pied* and the Italian calls it *il pede*. French-speaking Normans, Latin-speaking scientists and especially the high-class language of Shakespeare, are principally responsible for the large stock of Latin derivatives in the English language.

Derivatives of the word foot are of common use in daily life as football, footboard, footman, footpad, footgear, etc. The word "footfixer" would, however, be offensive to an educated chiropodist.

The words of preferable style pertaining to the foot are derived from the Latin word *pedes*, directly, or by the use of French roots. Reference is had to words like pedal, pedestal, pedestrian, biped, quadruped, expedite, impede, centipede, etc. *Pedicure* is, therefore, an old deserving word instead of Chiropody; but this word is scientifically incorrect because two Latin nouns cannot be properly combined to create a compound word.

Modern sciences prefer original Greek derivations for scientific words. Therefore the scientific English language contains many derivatives of the Greek word for foot. The second part of the word Chiropody is thus derived. Pseudopodia (untrue feet) is used as a substitute for "feet" in the class of protozoa, the simplest and lowest form of animal life. The many divisions and subdivisions in Zoology are named by derivatives of the Greek word *pus;* cephalopoda means headfooted, brachiopoda = armfooted, gastropoda = bellyfooted, skaphopoda = canoefooted, arthropoda = jointfooted, polypes, shortened from polypoda = manyfooted, myriapoda = tenthousandfooted, dekapoda = tenfooted, oktopoda = eightfooted, hexapoda = sixfooted, tetrapoda = fourfooted, bipoda = twofooted and apoda = footless. As explanatory of arthropoda, the other part of this word is arthron, meaning articulation. From the same root, arthritis is used by the medical profession as indicating inflammation of a joint. Arthritis urica means an arthritis caused by a deposit of uric acid. This condition is very often found on the large toe. The common name for arthritis is gout. In professional language it is termed *podagra,* meaning gout of the foot.

The Semitic languages are a family of languages in addition to the Aryan and the Hamitic. The Semitic languages were spoken in olden times in western Asia and the Hamitic languages were spoken in northern Africa. In modern times the Hamitic languages are largely replaced by the Semitic, particularly since the expansion of the Mohamedan. The Babylonian and Assyrian languages are of Semitic origin. We noted elsewhere that *shepu* was a word for foot. In Hebrew the foot is *régel;* most other Semitic languages use the same word root as is used in Hebrew. In Arabic *ridshul* means the foot; in Aramaic the word for foot is *ragla.* The letters *r* and *l* are interchangeable in many old languages. *Ligra* is the foot in old Syrian inscriptions and *ligra* is used to designate the foot in the Mandaic dialect.

Old Egyptian is a Hamitic language. The foot is there known as *red*. In some of the dialects of the Coptic language the foot is called *rat* and *let*.

The Aryan, Semitic and Hamitic languages belong together as a more or less close group. Isolated languages in Europe are spoken by the Basques, the Sardinians and the Albanians. A new group of languages noted in eastern Europe is the Turk-Tartarian. The Turkish (Osmanli), Hungarian, Finnish and Lapponic languages are spoken in Europe. Turk-Tartarian languages are most common in the northwest of Asia.

We merely mention these languages, but will not attempt further to consider them here philologically.

## THE WORDS FOR TOE

In most languages the word for finger is the same as is used to designate the toe of the foot. In the Aryan languages, the Germanic group is an exception to this rule. In this latter group the fingers and the toes are differentiated, as will be shown.

In ordinary conversation, where we employ English words of Germanic origin, the fingers and toes are discriminated. In the conversation of the more learned, the words of Latin origin are used and there this discrimination is absent The scientific designations in medicine and surgery which should discriminate fingers and toes are of Greek derivation; this is also so in the Latin language. The educated Podiatrist should have a knowledge of the word for finger in the different languages if he would be properly conversant with his work. *Dik-* or *dig-* (the hyphen shows a missing and variable suffix), is an old Aryan word root meaning "to show." The fingers of the hand are designated from this root in different Aryan languages as indicating instruments. Again the number of fingers on both hands led to the word *ten*, originating from the same root. The Greek *daktylos* (δάκτυλος) and the Latin *digitus*, both meaning finger, also come from this root. The later Roman languages still have derivates of this root as noted in the French word *le doigt*, which means finger as well as toe. *Daktylos* and *digitus* are used indiscriminately for finger and toe in the old Greek and Latin medical books, both before and after Christ.

The toe in anatomy is therefore called digitus. Greek derivatives of daktylos are used in pathology, as in *syndaktyly*, meaning joint toe and *hyperdaktyly*, meaning supernumerary toe. Not all of the Aryan languages employed the same word for fingers and toes. Some thousands of years ago the Celtic language held sway over the whole of western Europe This family belongs to the Aryan group. One of these subdivisions is the Gaelic idiom which is still spoken in Ireland. In this latter language, finger and toe (ɱέɑɲ) is derived from an entirely different word root.

The Semitic languages use derivatives from a common root to designate finger and toe. In old Babylonian and in old Assyrian the word is *sumbu*, in Hebrew and in western Aramaic it is *ezba* and in Arabian, Syrian and Abyssinian it is *issba*. Of the Hamitic group, the Old Egyptians called finger and toe *zeba* (hieroglyphic 𓂧), whereas in the different Coptic languages they were known as *tĕb*, *tēb* and *thĕb*. Hungarian is one of the Turk-Tartarian languages in which finger and toe is styled *ujj*. *Láb-újj* would express finger of foot; this combination must be used to differentiate the toe from the finger. Very many languages of the Pacific Ocean belong to the Malayan group; the Malgassian language, common to Madagascar, is one of these There finger is known as *rantsan*, differentiated as *rantsantanana*, finger of the hand, and *rantsan-tomboka* finger of the foot. Many languages have a special word for thumb. Where fingers and toes have a common name, the same word is used for thumb and big toe. The Irish-Gaelic uses όηοόϛ to designate both the thumb and the big toe. The Hebrew language of the Gospel likewise does not differentiate the word for thumb and big toe. The small finger also has at times a special designation. In Irish-Gaelic the small finger is called *luidin* and the small toe *luidin na coise;* the latter means small finger of the foot. In the Malgassian language, the little finger is called *anki-hely* or *ankisay*. The little toe, as a special expression, would be there called *anki-hely-tomboka* or *ankisay-tomboka*.

As stated in the history of the word foot, the Germanic family of languages is a branch of the Aryan group. The German language has a special word for finger as well as a special word for toe. The word finger is common to all of these languages and is cognate to the German root *fangen;* this means to catch. The root for the designation of toe is also a common one; but its origin is not thoroughly clear. Some linguists believe these words to be the cognate of the Latin "digitus;" others contend to the contrary. The existence of a word *daipa* or *daika* or *daiqua* must be presupposed as existing in some old aboriginal language. The law of sound displacing is mentioned above and would account for the change of the Greek word *pod* to the English word foot. The same reasoning would lead from the above presupposed word to the real known words of toe, etc., in the Germanic family of languages. The word toe is in each of the following languages as here stated: old Anglo-Saxon, *táhoe* and *tá;* old Icelandic, *tá;* Dutch, *teen;* English, *toe;* old High German *zéhá;* middle High German *zéhe;* new High German (language of the books) *zeh;* Bavarian slang, *zéchen;* Suevian slang, *zaichen;* Alemanien slang *zéb; zébe;* Franconian and Henneberg slang, *zéwe;* Thuringian slang, *ziwe*. If Germany were divided into separate kingdoms, as is the case with Holland, Denmark, Norway, Sweden and Finland, these slang words would attain the dignity of the words of independent languages. But linguists are not influenced by political situations and changes; therefore, slang or dialect is of the same significance as the accepted true language.

It is astonishing that in some German slang expressions the toes are called exactly the same as they were known to the oldest language of hieroglyphic inscriptions. It may be that all of the words for fingers and toes are cognate in the Aryan, Semitic and Hamitic languages. We will learn that the root of the word horn, explaining the designation *corn*, is another word common to these three groups; but such words are very rare and may belong to the stock of the oldest human aboriginal and common language. Most of these old words are lost by new formations in the mutations of time. Such new formations may readily be explained, as instanced in the Latin word "digitus" designating finger and toe. The early people of England used a plant which they called foxglove. The old Greek and old Roman books do not contain mention of this plant; but the modern Germans have a word *Fingerhut*, which in English means thimble. The modern scientists, a few centuries ago, translated digitalis as meaning thimble; but as a matter of fact digitalis is only a new coined word. Digitalis is now very much used in materia medica to replace what in olden times was known as *squilla*. Digitalis is far better known than foxglove. The word foxglove will be forgotten after a few centuries. And so it has happened that in the different languages, from century to century, new words were substituted, old words were lost and the sounds of existing words were displaced. If in a given language fingers and toes are designated by separate words, the word thumb can no longer include the idea of the big toe. But the big toe was not thought of enough importance to warrant the generation of a separate word or the conservation of an old one. In Latin the thumb is called *pollux* and the big toe *hallux;* but the English language has only "big toe," as the German language has only *grosse zehe*, to express the foot analogy to "thumb" and *daume*.

### THE WORDS FOR NAIL

The care of the nails of the fingers and of the toes is a very old branch of cosmetics and hygiene. No language is known to the writer in which different words are in use to designate the nails of the fingers on the hand in contradistinction to the nails of the toes. The Sumerian expression *dubbin* and the Babylonian *zupru*, differ very much from the root, which is recognizable through all the Aryan languages. In old Sumerian *nir* is the foot. An old Aryan root *nogh* or *nokh* may be cognate. In old Slavonian *noga* is foot, in Russian it is *noga* and in Polonian it is *nog*. But this Aryan root is not retained in its original sense in families of the Aryan languages other than in the Slavonic. It is ofttimes augmented by prefix and again by suffix. The customary general meaning of such new formations of this root has reference to something in connection with the foot, but frequently these words distinctly specify the nails. In Sanskrit *nakha* means finger or toe nails; this is similar in the Slavic languages. In Lithuanian, *nagas* means finger nail and *naga* means horse's hoof; in Old Slavonian *noguti* means nail or claw.

A vowel is prefixed to this root in the Mediterranian and in the Celtic language groups. Greek *onyx*, plural *onyches*, means claw, talon, hoof—also hook. This word also means stone of the same half translucent appearance as the human nails. Pathologic terms in regard to the nail must be derived from this word, in keeping with the scientific method previously stated.

*Onychia* means inflammation of the nail; *paronychia* (*para*—beside) means an inflammation next the nail. *Onychogryphosis* translated is "curvature of the nail," a not uncommon deformity of that appendage. *Onychomykosis* (the latter part of the word from *mykos*, mushroom) means sickness from fungi of the nail.

The Latin word of the same root is *unguis*, nail of toe, claw, talon. Irish-Gaelic, is *ionga* nail of fingers or toes; *ungula* is the Latin word for horse's hoof. In addition to the prefixed vowel above noted the word is enlarged in German by the suffixed "l." The nails of the fingers and toes in olden times were stained (generally yellow) to conform to the then style. This staining is still usual in some Oriental countries. The pigment now mostly used is henna. From this incident Latins used the word *unguere*, to anoint, and *unguentum*, ointment. The English word ointment is a derivative of "unguentum." As shown in the oldest languages of ancient times, an ointment was a preparation used only for manicure and pedicure purposes. This word acquired its broader meaning only in more modern times.

It is worthy of remark that the Celtic group of languages is the only Western group which has a special word for toe or finger nail, for the nail of carpentry and for the pathologic corn.

The Latin *ungula* leads to the French *l'ongle* the nail. The German language does not employ the prefixed vowel, but instead uses the suffixed "l"as seen in the Latin *ungula*; Gothic *nagls;* old Icelandian *nagl;* old Saxonian *nagal;* Anglo-Saxon *naegel;* English *nail;* Dutch *nagel;* old High German, *nagal;* Middle High German, *nagel;* Modern High German, *nagel.* Most of these words have the double meaning of nail of the finger or toe, and wooden or iron nail. But in old Icelandic there is a distinction between *nagl* as finger nail and *nagle* as the nail of carpentry.

Beside the Germanic family, the Aryan languages (other than the German group) never designate nails for mechanical use by the same word as they use for finger nails; but there is a common word sometimes used expressing both the meaning for the nails of commerce and the name for corns.

The learned physician, as part of his scientific armamentarium, has a knowledge of the Latin and Greek languages which should be pedantic. By this means he is enabled to give professional expression to his work in conformity with a combined knowledge of Latin, Greek and his native language. A traditional rule exists for the selection of the particular language to be employed. We called attention to this rule in our narration of the use of the words for foot, toe and nail. Later on we will, in the same way, collate and explain the etymology of "corns." This should be sufficient as a general introduction for the podiatrist to the scientific language of the profession of medicine. It should also show sufficiently the conception of prehistoric mankind in their nomenclature of the organs of the body. A thoroughly complete education in this sense contemplates the humanistic preparation of the physician for his life work. Some centuries, or even only decades ago, this education was a main requirement of every physician. The presence or absence of this character of preparation was also in Europe, until late years, the boundary line which separated the *chirurgus major* and the *chirurgus minor.* The natural sciences themselves are in more recent times estimated to be of major value. The requirements which contemplated scholastic attainments have been largely abandoned. But the well educated physician and surgeon still needs and will continue to require a broad education. The difference between the average surgeon and the chiropodist will become lessened if the chiropodist will acquire more of this liberal education. It would be sufficient, if the chiropodist were to know the history of his profession and the meaning of all words therein employed. The roots of a few words will primarily supply all that he needs in this particular, but as his knowledge increases he will refuse to be a chiropodist, but instead will aspire to be a scientific podiatrist.

### THE WORDS FOR FOOTWEAR

In every civilization of which footgear was a part, different kinds of footwear were made for different uses; each had its appropriate name. In modern times we have different layers of footwear. For the skin we have socks and stockings and beyond that we have shoes and boots. Where very thin socks or stockings are worn we sometimes have undersocks and oversocks and also, additionally to shoes, rubbers are sometimes worn. These different kinds of footwear each represent a different evolution; they differ according to countries, races of people and the cultivation which has come with the centuries. The fashions have changed through the years. These changes have, in the main, lead to faulty selection and to bad construction. To these circumstances the cause of pathologic conditions of the foot and especially the origin of corns is largely due.

Sandals are the simplest form of footwear. Professional sandalmakers were craftsmen known to ancient Egypt. They are mentioned in the Papyros Ebers, one of the oldest medical books in existence. The transcription of the above hieroglyphic is *tbw*. The different Coptic languages are derivatives of the old Egyptian; they use letters very similar to those of the Greeks. TOOYE and ΘΩΟΥΙ, the sandalmaker, are pronounced *tŏwĕ* and *thōwi*. The first of these hieroglyphics represents a sandal with straps. This word looks in some way familiar to the previously mentioned Egyptian expression for toes. The word sandal is of Greek origin; the Latin name is soleae. In the old Greek language pedilon (πέδιλον) is an expression for all footwear, but the old Greeks used sandals almost exclusively and therefore *pedilon* is also translated as sandal. Sandals of a sole only are today used by the Americans and the English—in fact by most Europeans as well. These modern sandals are copied from the Japanese. Slippers are practically sandals with toe covering. In German, slippers are called *pantoffel*, from the Italian word *pantofola*, which has the same meaning. This word is known in Germany only since the fifteenth century. The most common word for the entire Germanic family of languages for regular footwear is "shoe" and its cognates. Footgear, covering the entire foot and reaching up over the lower limb, is in English styled "boot," German, *stiefel*. The history of this latter word is very interesting. *Stig* in Icelandic means "a step" and *vjel* in the same language means a machine, engine, artifice, craft, device, fraud. The word *stigvjel*, as boot, is still used in Iceland, literally meaning an artificial construction for walking. The Normans used this word and it became in Italian *stivale*, boot; a second adaption led to the German word *stiefel*, also meaning boot.

The separate use of stockings and hose is only of recent origin. The French expression for stocking was *bas de chausses*. Stockings were originally sewn from leather or woolen cloth and were directly connected with the pants. Knitted, separated stockings were introduced only in the sixteenth century and first in England. Tradition states that Queen Elizabeth was the first to use these separated stockings.

### THE FOOT IN ZOOLOGY AND IN COMPARATIVE ANATOMY

The difference between animal and plant is in the main, that the animal can, of its own motion, change its place whereas the plant does not possess this faculty. Very few kinds of animals lose the power of spontaneous locomotion by secondary adaptation. The organs of locomotion of animals are called feet. In zoology the feet are under all circumstances the most important organs of the system. The *protozoa* the simplest animals, consisting only of one cell, do not have true feet, but they can spontaneously create excrescences of living tissue; we call these *pseudopodia*, which means apparent feet. Nor do the *echinodermata* have true feet.

The *coelenterata* are usually fixed as to their position. This latter group includes the *polypes* (which means manyfooted), whose foot-like appendices around the mouth help to catch the food which they ingest. As we proceed to higher organized animals, we come in contact with groups in which the feet are partly or entirely changed to organs of mastication; to organs of respiration; or to organs of generation. *Vermes* are the lowest order of animals with rudimentary feet for locomotion. The *arthropoda* have very highly organized and very well articulated feet. They include the *crustacea*, with a main group the *decapoda* (crawfishes, lobsters, crabs, etc.), the *myriapoda* (English, thousandlegs), the *arachnoidea* (spiders and similar animals with eight legs), and the *hexapoda* (insects with six feet). This group of insects has very many subdivisions and numerous special representatives. Amateurs frequently collect one or the other of the above in their first studies of natural history. The next group, the mollusca, is divided into *lamellibranchiata, scaphopoda, gastropoda* and *cephalopoda.* Shells of molluscs are also frequently collected at the sea-shore by students of natural history. The molluscoidea are divided in *brachiopoda* and *bryozoa,* which latter are subdivided and designated according to the character of the feet.

The vertebrate animals have four extremities identical with the human hands and feet. In their places the fishes have four fins. Amphibia, reptilia and mamalia, as a rule, have four feet; however, some amphibia and reptilia are footless, as, for instance, the snakes. The bird creation have wings in the place of the fore feet; while human beings have hands in the place corresponding to fore feet and to wings.

Beside the fishes, all other vertebrates start the development of the feet with five toes or five fingers. Some of these five toes may become crippled, attenuated or may even entirely disappear in certain families of animals. This circumstance assists greatly in the systematizing of zoology. The placental mammalia are divided into the group which stands on the whole foot and into another group which stands on the tips of the toes only. The toe nails of the latter group become transformed into hoofs; during this transformation one or more of the original toes disappear. Thus, we have the manyhoofed, the twohoofed and the onehoofed animals, in which latter groups the horse and cattle belong.

As the feet of mammalia are split into toes, so the claws of crabs have a scissorlike termination and the legs of insects have two talons. The human thumb is opposed to the four other digits of the hand, but the human big toe does not bear a like relationship to the other digits of the foot. The big toes of the monkeys and the claws of crabs show the same relationship of the big toe to the other digits as the human thumb shows to the fingers of the hand. The organs of locomotion in this way became transformed into mediums of offense and defense. The morphology of the feet is a special and very important branch of scientific zoology. The feet of animals are their most vulnerable parts; they are exposed.

The partial or total loss of one or more feet has no great significance in cases where animals have many feet. Notwithstanding this circumstance nature has afforded this lower form of animals with protection for their feet. The feet of arthropoda are plated by *chitin*. This covering is from time to time stripped off, casting the skin and then, until the normal condition of affairs is restored, such animals for days at a time, sequester themselves. The trunks of turtles, armadillos and hedgehogs are protected by hard coverings. In such, the feet may be withdrawn so as to be hidden from view.

The terminating toes of the feet of all vertebrates are plated by nails. In other cases the feet are protected against danger in a supplementary and augmented manner. Hornplates cover the skin of the feet of crocodiles and birds. The cock has a spur on the back of his leg corresponding anatomically and histologically to a gigantic corn. This spur may develop to such an extent as to generate a bone in the axis joint of the skeleton; it is the most dangerous weapon of the cock. There is not a place on the skin of other higher animals, where such an accidental corn could not be generated. Sometimes they are physiologic, sometimes pathologic. To this group belong the horns of cattle, antelopes, goats, sheep, giraffes, the tissue on the nose of the rhinoceros; the bill of the kasuar and of other birds is of similar anatomic construction. Such pathologic "horns" are also known to horses, cats, wolves, geese, ducks and chickens.

Every part of the skin of higher animals may be subjected to pressure and to rubbing. Where this occurs nature, as a matter of self protection, automatically creates there a thickened cornlike welt as a buffer. Civilized mankind is also exposed to these conditions and thus many opportunities arise where nature imposes these welts. The human skin is usually covered by clothing of soft material; is scantily covered with hair and is ordinarily very thin. Handicraftsmen who are continuously using shovels, hoes, picks and hammers acquire welts on the hands. The heloma, or common English corn, is only a special kind of welt caused by the pressure of ill-fitting footgear; it is a natural consequence. Because of its position, the welt which forms on the foot and is commonly classed as a "corn," is exceptionally painful. Most other welts are usually painless.

The feet and other extremities stand out apart from the trunk. They contain none of the more important organs of life. The trunk contains the central nerve system, the central blood system, the central respiration system, the central resorption system, the central excretion system and the generation organs. All this is centralized in the human species and in most animals. Only in insects and in birds do the organs of locomotion and respiration have a closer relationship. In many, feet, hands, skin, and morphology are developed in the closest relationship, but are separated from the above mentioned primary important organs.

The care and treatment of these central organs are exclusively the province of the graduated and licensed physician. Again, if there be any diseases of the feet, the hands, the skin, or of the body stature which are of systemic origin, the physician alone is competent to care for them. The major surgery of the foot is the exclusive province of the surgeon. If local treatment is required, the "chirurgus minor" is competent and thus the chiropodist enters the field of activity and of usefulness  In these latter cases the minor surgeon very often finds it necessary to observe special care in order to conserve the beauty of the body. Simple local medical and surgical treatment is often possible, to preserve life and health, but where the most important point for the patient is the preservation of beauty, the regular physician and the regular surgeon are very often less competent to aid than is he who scientifically specializes along these lines. The physician possesses no training and no experience in this character of work; it is the kingdom where the science of cosmetic rules.

Kosmos is a Greek word which originally meant ornament; later it acquired the meaning of "nice arrangement" and also "the well arranged world." The medieval period typified the whole world as *makrokosmos*, meaning "the large world," and the human body as *mikrokosmos*, meaning "the small world." The Greek words *makros*, large, and *mikros*, small, are also used in *makroskopy*, meaning the contemplation by the naked eye, showing only the large things, and in *mikroskopy*, meaning the contemplation by the microscope, which reveals very small things. *Kosmetics* is the science to create or to conserve the beauty of the human body.

Cosmetics may be divided into four or five special branches. The first branch of Cosmetics comprehends the field of the present text-book, the cosmetics of the foot, properly termed "Podiatry" or "Chiropody." The second branch is the cosmetic treatment of the hands. This is now known as manicuring; when scientifically developed this branch might properly be styled *Chir-*

*iatry*. A third branch would relate to the skin, *Dermatiatry*, and a fourth branch would treat of the hair, *Komiatry*. The fifth branch is the care of the teeth. The scientific name would be *Odontiatry*. This branch of cosmetics has long since become a scientific profession, but they still call it by the unscientific name of *Dentistry*. The special cosmetic treatment of the teeth has been lately developed and is called *Orthodontia*. The other four cosmetic branches should have their scientific development at some college set apart for that purpose.

The personal impression of the writer is, that the School of Chiropody of New York is only the nucleus of a college of cosmetics which will later on accord scientific instruction in all of the above branches. Chiropody or Podiatry cannot be absolutely separated in the introductory chapters of this work from the other cosmetic branches. In olden times they were united. The most famous cosmetic practitioner of ancient times was the well known Egyptian Queen, Kleopatra. She wrote a text-book on cosmetic practice. The famous physician Galenos copied some chapters from this work and these are the only ones which have been preserved, all else having been lost. This fact is very much to be regretted as it creates an unhappy gap in the history of podiatry.

The podiatrist will find much in relation to his profession that is worthy of serious study, the pursuit of which will enable him to help raise the standard of his calling. He should be closely in touch with the contingent sciences; should carry on his practice as a specialist in a limited field, but he should extend his studies far beyond the boundaries of his professional work.

### THE ABORIGINAL HISTORY OF PODIATRY

We must turn to the animal creation to find the starting point of the cosmetic care of the feet. Thousands of so-called "fiddlers" are seen in summer time in the bay meadows near the seashore vigorously and assiduously cleaning their front feet from residues of food. Many birds and many mammalia execute a similar recurrent treatment of their skin, feathers and hair. An easy object of observation is the cat. The cat goes to a tree or to a stake; she rises and stretches; alternately the extended feet are made to claw the wood and are then withdrawn with claws drawn. It would seem as though she were sharpening her nails. Continuous observation shows that the nails are in this **manner** lost, to be replaced by a newer nail growth. Such is an example of spontaneous podiatry common to the cat family.

An insufficient understanding of the habits of animals by man can be noted from the following: A short time ago the nails of the big tiger in the museum in Central Park became too large; it was necessary to cut them and the operation was performed. If this tiger could have had a chance to follow his natural custom, this operation would have been unnecessary. In the forest nobody else cares for the nails of the tiger; he does his own manicuring. The cat also, in every-day experience, accumulates dirt between her toes. She removes this by licking; sometimes a firmer material gathers between her toes and sticks to the hair; then we may observe that the animal uses her teeth to remove this foreign substance.

We have referred to the group of mammalia which stands on the ends of the toes. In such cases the nails are transformed to hoofs and thus become very important parts of the anatomy. Nails, hoofs and hair consist chemically of the same keratin as do the corns. Corns are derived ontogenetically and anatomically from the same embryonic tissue as nails, hoofs, teeth and hair. Nails and hair are merely transmutations by heredity of original corn tissue. If you go to any zoologic garden, as in New York, to the Bronx or to Central Park, you will see the different genera of monkeys, most of them having red colored welts in the gluteal region. These welts arise from their continuous sitting on these naked parts and may be properly called normal physiologic corns of a special character acquired by hereditary tendencies.

Corns pathologically are, therefore, individual nails, hair, welts or horns produced by chronic local irritation. This circumstance is also an added reason for considering cosmetics a science which should comprehend the care of the skin, of the hair, of the teeth, of the nails and of all characters of horny excrescences. These tissues are uniform in the bodies of sharks. The higher vertebrates have differentiated them. The farther the differentiation has gone, the greater the need for a differentiated care. The human being, as the highest developed, needs the most care. Specialization along these lines is therefore essential.

The nails of the toes of cattle and of pigs are of the split hoof variety. The horse has only conserved the middle finger or toe of every foot. The respective four nails are transformed as simple hoofs. The horse practices but very little instinctive care of his hoofs. Only stamping and scraping is permitted him to aid nature in caring for his feet. The lower end of the horse's hoof as it becomes worn, is replaced by new like tissue from above.

Man, as the owner and user of horses, long ago recognized the importance of suitable hoof care. The farrier is a very important man as assistant to the horse trainer. There is a long list of disorders and diseases of the horse hoof treated by the experienced blacksmith. The horse shoer is also a preserver of the horse-hoof. The blacksmith who understands shoeing and hoof care, is of a higher order than the average blacksmith. He practices the podiatry of horses.

We can not go into farther details, but every expert on horses will state that the care of the horses' hoofs has equal value with the combined surgery and medication of horses. The care of the feet of the cavalry horse in military life is of equal importance to the health of his rider.

It seems strange and even ludicrous, in the light of these explanations, that the scientific podiatry of the human foot is in its infancy. But this merely seems to be so. If we go back to the earliest history of man we will find that there has always existed a high appreciation of the need for care of the human foot. The pictures of the human foot, as characterized by hieroglyphics and illustrations in previous pages demonstrate the truth of this contention. Other incidents give the same impression. Between the podiatry of ancient times and the resurrected foot care of today in its scientific garb, there has come the shoe as a covering to the human foot. A consideration of this phase of so-called development is essential to the work in hand.

## THE GENERAL HISTORY OF SHOES

There are many books containing contributions to the history of shoes. In the last century the writings of Meyer, Günther, Starcke, Knöfel, Rodegast and Franke are in evidence. It is only within the last few decades that we have been enabled to study the history of this subject as it applied to the civilized people of very remote times. History shows that at one and the same time in certain ancient countries, there were those who wore sandals and others who wore shoes, and again those who went about with bare feet. The conclusion must be that these forms of footgear varied at different times in the same countries and that some inventions of shoes were of an independent nature. Three main reasons that led to the invention of shoes and the need for their use are found by a study of the history of the times: (1) Dangers from ice and snow in the winter time; (2) the possibility of wounds from thorns and stones in hunting; and (3) the necessity for protection of the feet for distant trips of warriors. Luxurious ladies were also interested in wearing shoes for the purpose of conserving the skin of the feet so that it might be thin and beautiful to look upon.

The monuments of old Egypt reveal to us the most ancient history available. No rain damaged the pictures on the walls of these tombs. The oldest monuments of Babylonia may be equally old, and it is also not improbable that some Babylonian ruins may be even older than the oldest exemplars in Egypt. In Babylonia, such wall pictures are not preserved as they have been in Egypt. Therefore, to get our bearings we have to start from the earliest times of old Egypt. African, Asiatic and European peoples are in some instances depicted with all of the true details of habit.

When we examine the pictures of the Babylonian region of later times, the details as to dress are less pronounced. As we proceed farther in historic research we may perhaps be able to add to our resources of this nature. There is one grave difficulty in the study of shoes from the monuments of the past. It was improper in the old Orient for men in the humbler walks of life to wear shoes in the presence of those of more exalted rank. The king, as monarch, was there the mentor of all. The king and the gods are represented in the most of their pictures. Subjects of the ruling monarch, and even ambassadors of foreign subject countries, are there pictured without shoes or sandals. For them to wear a foot covering in the presence of royalty would have been an offense. The king alone could wear shoes or sandals, but that was forbidden even him when he was worshipping the gods. The gods in turn are represented without shoes; they do not need shoes, because neither thorn nor stone could hurt them.

Among the soldiery, only those especially favored had the right to wear sandals, shoes or garters in the presence of the king. The common soldier had this right only when acting as a sentinel. All this was the custom of the entire Orient. This is verified in many places in the gospels. The priest must be barefooted, if worshipping. According to the gospel, God cried from the burning thornbush to the patriarch: "First take off thy shoes!" The husband of Elizabeth is enforced, barefooted, to render sacrifice in the Temple. There is also the law of the levirate in the gospel: if the brother-in-law refused to marry the widow of his brother, she had the right to take off his shoes in the presence of the magistrates. This was an infamation; because a wife did for him what in common life only a man in higher station could do for him.

In the oldest Babylonian times the king Gudea and other kings and princes of the same period were represented as barefooted. Similar pictures of times very much later are in evidence. These latter, however, may be merely imitations of ancestral practices and not evidences of what actually happened at the time they were made. As a rule kings and princes are represented as worshipping. King Naramsin is the most ancient Asiatic whom the writer has found represented as wearing sandals. We have pictures of later periods, representing scenes in royal palaces. There the kings wear sandals and also shoes.

The shoe-wearing soldier on duty in the presence of the king is proof of the following idea: The shoe of the citizen was deemed a luxury, the shoe of the busy warrior, a necessity. The indigenous Egyptian of every period in history did not care to be a soldier. The long extent of country ran from North to South and in the East and West it was protected by the desert. There was never either snow nor ice. The ground was precipitated slime from the river and was free of stones. There was no need of shoes. The common people there retained the barefoot habit for centuries and centuries.

The history of the period from 4000 or 3000 before Christ to about 1500 before Christ is fairly well known. There are innumerable proofs of changes in dress, changes in hair wear and changes in styles of jewelry; but, from the lowest laborer to the highest royal functionary, the entire people remained barefooted. This applies also to the most fashionable women, even though their meetings and entertainments seem on occasions to have been very much like the most up-to-date functions of modern times.

Many foreign peoples came in contact with the old Egyptians and have a place in these wall pictures. Many different kinds of shoes can be there noted. The inhabitants of Africa, the negroes of the interior of Africa, as well as the Ethiopians of the sea shore bearing the incense tree, are always represented in bare feet. The king himself was always barefooted, but from the ankle to the knee his right leg was encircled with large copper rings. Such was the practice in Africa many thousands of years ago and it remains so until today.

In Egypt, before 1500 B.C., the use of sandals was rare. At that time they began to come into use. The earliest footgear there noted has a strap running from both sides of the heel across the upper part of the tarsus; there it joined a second strap, starting between the big toe and the second toe. Later on the sandals acquired a marginal strip and still later a marginal wall of leather. This marginal wall led to the development of the real shoe. During all of this period, Egypt was in continuous connection and in cultural exchange with all other Mediterranean countries. The Egyptians estimated sandals and shoes as far from comfortable. Possibly they wore them merely to be considered in style. But decency was conserved, if the Egyptian gentleman of quality went barefooted, provided a special slave followed his master bearing the latter's shoes in his hands. Thus also was comfort and propriety satisfied.

The ancient Arabian, because of his rough and stony country, developed different ideas on this subject. The Arabian warrior, (2000 B. C.) never wore shoes; but high-class Arabian travellers, living at about this time (the twelfth Egyptian dynasty) wore a special kind of traveller's shoes, in the form of sandals of black leather. In these, the dorsum pedis was covered by a reticular arrangement of straps. The Arabian ladies of this time wore real, seemingly comfortable, shoes of red leather constructed so as to barely reach up to the ankles. They were set off with a sort of cuff made of some white material.

The Semites who lived in the towns of the southwest, at about the same time, wore shoes similar to those common to the Arabian Bedouins. The shoes worn by the women and the children were, however, somewhat higher. It would seem that this footgear was only a luxurious habit of the most prominent of the non-male population. The Syrian tribes are the oldest inhabitants of northern Arabia and the pictures of them show that even when they were engaged in warfare they went barefooted.

The powerful Kingdom of the Chetites, which practically perished about 1000 B.C., was more civilized than most of the other tribes of Northern Syria and Asia Minor. The remnants of this nationality are evidenced in other later empires such as the Phrygians and the Lydians, but more especially in the Jewish kingdom of Saul, David and Solomon in the city of Jerusalem.

There probably is no modern Jew who has not some of the blood of the Chetites flowing in his veins.

The shape of the modern shoes is in a large percentage of cases derived from the old Chetitic shoes. The ruins of the capital of the Chetites are in the neighborhood of the village Boghaz-Köi in the Taurus mountains. Hugo Winckler, of Berlin, a personal friend of the writer, dug out from these ruins many cuneiform inscriptions and there contracted the illness which led to his death. The Chetites are always pictured wearing the characteristic boots of Asia Minor. These boots cover one-half the calf of the leg and are curved upward in the part where the toes rest. Such boots are depicted in the drawings of the Kyprian and the Kilikian people. The shoes of the Etrurians, the oldest civilized people of Italy, are similar. The Turshas, an invading foreign nation of Egypt, contemporaneous with the Etrurians, wore the same beak-like shoes. These shoes are preserved by the Karpaths of Eastern Europe, the Finns, the Eskimos, the Swedes and the Norwegians. In the interior of Asia are many different tribes of Mongolians. They have been isolated from western civilization until very recent years; therefore it is that only recently has it been learned that the footgear of these people is and has been similar in the main, to that of the Chetites of centuries before them. The style of this footgear is most hurtful to the feet and probably was the most fruitful cause of corns and callosities among the Caucasian races; therefore, their consideration will be taken up later.

The oldest civilization of which we know is the Babylonian. It includes all the nations that ever used cuneiform inscriptions for writing. The shoes of the Babylonians were entirely different from those worn by the Arabians and the Chetites. The oldest Arabian shoes were constructed for and worn by travellers. The Chetitic shoes are hunters' shoes and shoes intended for districts in which snow and ice were common. The Babylonian, and especially the Assyrian shoes, were of the variety suitable to the warrior. The original Assyrian shoes were simple sandals from which there was a special characteristic development.

It was the custom of Arabic and other warriors of ancient times to sever the tendo Achillis of children and of beasts of burden in the country of the enemy. The purpose was to cripple the children so that they might never be fit for warfare and to render the animals unfit for use for similar purposes The vulnerability of this sinew is a theme of importance in Greek mythology and in the German mythology of medieval times. The old Assyrian warriors were very anxious to protect this sinew. From the simple sandals they developed shoes with high vertical edges to protect the heel. This vertical strip of leather became smaller and smaller at its forward end until it entirely disappeared at the toe end of the foot. This half sandal —half shoe foot covering is frequently represented on Babylonian and Assyrian monuments of different times and is the predecessor of the low closed shoe previously mentioned as in use among the women and children of the Arabian Bedouins. A similar shoe for males was also sometimes used in Assyria. The Assyrian king Assarhaddon, the father of Sardanapal, in one old representation, wears such short shoes, the upper leather being magnificently ornamented. The representation of the Kilikians, as seen on old Egyptian monuments, shows the shape of the shoes worn by Assarhaddon. It would seem as though the sandal were made of elastic leather rather than the hard leather used in making the sandals worn by the Assyrian warriors. No special upper-leather was sewed to it, but the elastic leather extended beyond the plantar pedis sufficiently to cover the main part of the dorsum pedis and was retained there by from 6 to 8 parallel straps, thus giving the entire covering the shape and the appearance of a slipper. This form of shoe was worn more particularly by the Aryan Persians.

The shinbone is very much exposed to injury. Narrow meshes of laces afford greater protection to this part than would a covering of thin leather. Assyrian, Babylonian and Persian soldiers of later times wore a shoe similar to that of the Kilikians. The toes were free. From the heel to the calf there was a protecting piece of leather; but the dorsum pedis and the shinbone were protected by connecting laces.

The people of the countries mentioned in the Bible, as the gravings on monuments prove, as a rule, wore no shoes. Feet covered by shoes are especially mentioned in Exodus 3, 5; Josuah 5, 15; and Jesaiah 20, 2. At home, these people always were with bare feet. To cover the feet is, in the gospel, an euphemistic expression for defecation as only those indulging in this necessary act ever sat down and drew a covering over their feet. The shoe of olden times in northwestern Europe differed from the Assyrian warrior shoe in that the foot is in the main covered by a cloth fabric to protect it from unwholesome weather conditions. The body of the shoe is made of wood, the heel being free and the toes covered. These wooden shoes are still used by the inhabitants of the mountainous regions between Bavaria and Bohemia; also by dwellers in the German Alps, principally those at work in stables. They are also still in common use in some parts of Alsatia, in Denmark, in France, and still more frequently in Holland. Dutch pictures have again recently become popular; in these prints one can recognize this character of shoes as foot coverings for youths of both sexes. These shoes keep the feet very warm; they are used only on the street and in the stable. At home, in church, or when visiting, the wooden shoe is left standing before the door. When in the house, they wear only socks and these latter often have a duplicated sole. The custom of the Japanese is similar.

Throughout the whole northern regions in most ancient times, shoes with heels uncovered and closed toes were common, probably due to the severity of the climate and the presence of snow and ice. The ski is a shoe made of a very long piece of elastic wood. It bears the weight of the body, and when worn in traversing fields of snow by those skilled in their use, it is a simple matter to glide and step along with alacrity without danger of sinking. There are other varieties of snow shoes which are used in the various northern countries and climes.

The Babylonian, Assyrian and Persian empires at one time extended to Central Asia and to India. Zippelius, of Würzburg, a friend of the writer, has demonstrated that foot protection in those countries was not confined to the human, but that in times of war their horses were similarly cared for. Horseshoeing had its birth there because in these countries it was not uncommon to place in the roadways, travelled by the enemy, iron devices of spike formation, so as to injure the feet of man and horse; they well knew that a warrior or his horse whose feet were maimed was a useless factor in warfare. The Mediterranean people of classic times also used this method for rendering man and beast useless as war factors. The fords of rivers were especially dangerous in this respect. It is possible that the shoe with the upturned toe was originally intended as a protection from the dangers of the metal-pointed menace to the travelling warrior. Warriors in these early times wore boots, and later on their horses' shoes were of metal. The oldest horseshoes were made so as to cover the entire hoof. Later on, men and horses wore foot covering in times of peace as well, but only those were so habited as were likely at any time to engage in warfare. It is only comparatively recently that men and horses, without regard to war, began to wear shoes. The higher classes in monarchies liked to present the appearance of being warriors. Old Roman history teaches us that even as a boy the emperor Caligula wore warrior boots. From this peculiarity of foot wear he received his name, Caligula, meaning "a small boot."

The Greeks and Romans were not aboriginal inhabitants of the Mediterranean countries. They immigrated about 1000 B.C. from the north and they came even later. At this period people went barefooted. Their predecessors in Greece and Italy wore beak shoes. The prominent Greek and Roman women contracted the Oriental habit of wearing sandals. Later on the Greek and Roman men used sandals in the city streets and in travelling, but never on solemn occasions. These Greek and Roman sandals were usually simple soles of wood or of leather. They were fixed to the feet by means of complicated connecting straps, and with women, buckles were added over the instep, for adornment. At the same time they also wore shoes with free toes and with protected heels, the two flanks being connected by pieces of leather or by smaller laces. This was a remnant of Asiatic influence.

The Laponics and the Eskimos in the far north always required and wore full shoes. The imminent danger in their countries was that the toes would freeze. In Germany swelling of the joints of the toes and other lesions were common, due to the effects of the winter's cold. They always wore full shoes, especial care being observed to so construct them as to protect the toes. These districts may have generated the original beak shoes. The old nations of Asia Minor and of the Mediterranean countries, where these beak shoes were worn, may have been only the most southern spurs of a northern Turk-Tartarian group of people. Probably they wore their aboriginal shoes not only to protect them from the dangers of ice and snow, but also as a useful protection in war and in hunting.

The most complete history of culture is preserved in Egypt. In the later periods of the Roman and Greek empires, men wore warrior boots and women wore their special kind of soft shoes. At this time the Egyptians (or, as subsequently known, the Copts) increased their use of the shoe. In remote times sandals were made of papyrus. In northeastern Africa they now weave real shoes from papyrus, just as the Spaniards use *esparto*, the Bohemians *reed*, and the Russians *bast*, for the same purpose. Women's shoes, about 2000 B.C., were as stated, far different from those in use for men at that time. This difference persists even to this day, nor has it been noted that the female suffragists ever demanded an equality in the foot gear of the sexes. In olden times men wore shoes to protect the feet—women to adorn them; today men and women alike use them for both purposes.

The original inhabitants of all parts of America wore soft foot coverings. Among the Indians, dwelling in the Eastern woodland area, these shoes were known as "moccasins" and were made of animal pelts. The evidence is clear, from exhibits in the American Museum of Natural History, that the prehistoric

PRE-COLUMBIAN PERUVIAN SANDAL (INCA POTTERY)
*Printed here through the kindness of the Museum of Natural History New York N Y*

Indian of America wore sandals. The existence of sand flies, mosquitoes, poison-charged snakes, thorns, etc., created a greater need for foot protection among the American Indians than was necessary on the part of the aborigines of the mother countries.

The new arrival in the western part of the United States is still classed as a "tenderfoot." The reader may notice that this is not a scientific expression, nor is it manufactured ex cathedra; nor is it of Greek origin; it is real American English. As a matter of fact, the feet are the most misused part of the body. From the landing of the Pilgrim Fathers to the emigrant of today, the American city resident has to use his feet prodigiously. Going barefooted, as we were wont to in the old country, is quite impossible in America. Even the Ethiopian resident in the United States wears shoes. Such was never his custom through all the ages of African history. The Americans of today wear European modeled shoes, most of which are the derivates of the old beak shoes. The moccasin is a memory, excepting as a few members of former American Indian tribes cling to their ancestral customs as to foot covering.

## THE HISTORY OF BEAK SHOES

Beak shoes, from the evidences of monuments of the time, were first used about 2000 B.C., as the footgear of the Chetites in Asia Minor. The inhabitants of northwestern Europe, in the early history of civilization, had contact neither with Egyptians nor Babylonians. Therefore, it is perhaps that from the original district in which the wooden slipper was first worn, no people are pictured in Egyptian and Babylonian monuments. The people of all European countries known to the Egyptians and to the Babylon ans before 1000 B.C., wore some kind of beak shoes. Outside of the districts where wooden slippers were worn, beak shoes are still used in all the remote mountainous regions of Europe. This is especially so among the Karpathians dwelling on the borders of Austria, Roumania and Russia. In the north, the Finns, the Laplanders, the Swedes and the Norwegians still use the aboriginal beak shoes. The oldest kinds of beak shoes had no special sole leather and no special heels. In olden times the leather was very often made from the skin of the head of an animal. It was often untanned and in these countries it is still frequently used for similar purposes in the same way. The old stories of Ireland also make mention of such untanned shoes, designating them by a special name. The skin of these beak shoes extends below the plantar pedis and is united above the foot, covering the foot and also the lower part of the leg. The shape of the shoe is conserved by sewing the parts together. In the upper parts, the shoe is fixed by straps attached to the foot and to the crus pedis. This upper part of the shoe is to this day often decorated by red and yellow flaps; 4000 years ago the old Chetites used these very same kind of red and blue flaps, demonstrating a custom which has prevailed for 4000 years, during which period the maps of the country, the flags and even their religions underwent material changes. Such a custom may indeed be stated to be fixed.

Some years ago the writer of this article wore Finnish shoes during the winter months. These shoes were made from the untanned skin of the head of a reindeer. The hairs were still in evidence on the outside of the shoe. The hardest part of the leather is used to build the point of this style of shoe. Near to the point, the shoe becomes narrower and curves upward. This curved formation is very useful in shoes without separated soles because the material does not wear out as quickly at the toe end of the shoe. In the far north where skis are used, the feet are strapped to the wooden body of the shoe. The curved point is also a characteristic of the old Chetitic shoe. Of course, there was no occasion for the use of skis in Asia Minor; snow and ice were practically unknown factors in the daily life of the inhabitants of this country.

In the history of shoes there are, of course, many missing links. It were, however, well to mention here a very old kind of shoe that was worn by the women of China. These had real soles of leather which were sewed on and were far different from the Chetitic shoes previously mentioned. The toe part of these Chinese shoes also pointed upwards, proving that the style was one of custom and not of utility. The Chinese practice restriction of growth in the feet of young girls. Their feet are encased in shoes much too small to admit of normal growth and in consequence the foot of the stylish woman of that country is more like a horse's hoof than a human foot and is almost useless for regular walking. This custom leads to the fair presumption that the beak shoe was the shoe of the old Turk-Tartarian peoples dwelling north of the old country. The Laplanders and the Finns retained the Turk-Tartarian languages as well as the Turk-Tartarian shoes. The Karpathians may have lost their original language, just as their Turk-Tartarian neighbors, the Bulgarians, lost theirs and adopted the Slavonic tongue; however, it seems likely that the mountaineers used and retained the original form of shoe worn by their forefathers. Beak shoes were sometimes used in the Byzantine Empire and these same shoes ruled the mode of western Europe from the twelfth to the fifteenth century. The boundary inhabitants of Europe and Asia may have adopted the style of shoe common to the women of China, but there is no proof of this. In many countries language and religion changed, but the style of foot covering was retained through centuries.

The district where the beak shoes prevailed is very important in tracing the history of chiropody. Wearers of such shoes were afforded insufficient space for their toes and the latter, being crowded together, created all kinds of foot woes. Therefore, districts in which these shoes were first worn are naturally to be considered as the aboriginal districts of corns. Herodotus particularly mentions the Paphlagones wearing νέοιλα ἐπιχώριω ἐς μέσην κνήμην ἀνατείνοντα. This means that the Paphlagonian travellers' shoes reached to the calf of the leg. This remark of the Greek father of history proves that in his time the civilized district in which beak shoes were worn was limited and that the true Hellenes, more particularly, did not wear them at all. In western Asia Minor, Egyptian monuments show (about 1500 B. C.) some Lykian tribes wearing sandals. At this time sandals were there the exception even though noted in this historic manner. A thousand years later sandals drove out the beak shoes and the wearing of the latter became exceptional.

Contemporaneous with the Mykenae period, were the rulers who lived before the Hellenes in Greece and the Etrurians who lived in Italy before the Romans. The older inhabitants of both of these countries whose languages were unknown, are known to have worn beak shoes. The Hellenes and Romans immigrated later on, about 1000 B. C., into districts on the Mediterranean Sea. Hellenes and Romans are Aryans and never wore beak shoes; they banished them. We have also no indication of beak shoes having been worn by the old Germans, by the old Celts, by the old inhabitants of Spain or by the English.

The boundaries of language groups are not fixed because many peoples lost their primitive languages in the events of history. The Negroes of the United States will never become Caucassians, but they speak only English, an Aryan language, which is of Caucassian origin. Their physical body retains the original race characteristics even though their language has changed. The old Egyptians reproduced very clearly the lines of their ethnologic character, as well as their skin color, the latter ofttimes being displayed in an exaggerated manner. The Caucassians are depicted as white, the Ethiopians are pictured as black, the male Egyptians are painted brown and the female Egyptians are made to appear as yellow. In these monuments the representatives of the principal nations wearing beak shoes were always painted pink colored. They were not members of the Aryan nor of the Semitic nations. Were they Mongolians? Members of this race were Finns, Hungarians and Turks from the viewpoint of language. Monuments bearing a characteristic kind of inscription, not yet deciphered, are imputed to the Chetites. Some of the cuneiform excavations of Hugo Winckler were written in the internationally used Semitic-Babylonian language. We do not know the Chetitic language and cannot locate it, but the monuments of Boghaz-Köi, the capital of the old Chetitic empire, invariably present the characteristic beak shoe. Either the details are originally not represented or they are altogether lost, the colors being weatherbeaten.

The nations of Kefto and Mannus, as depicted in Egyptian monuments, wore a similar shoe. The excavations of Schliemann show that the predecessors of the Hellenes in Troy (Asia Minor) and Cyprus were presumably Keftos and Mannus. The Homeric heroes must have been of this nationality. Menelaos, Agamemnon, and Hektor probably wore shoes of this kind. These nations inhabited eastern Asia Minor and were the southwestern neighbors of the Chetites. They are pictured as red men. Possibly these nations have some relation to the Bulgars or to the Albanians. Paphlagonia may have been only a part of this old kingdom, especially the northern part, which contained the most mountains. The Hellenes styled these Paphlagonians as rustics and conservatives. They may have been merely a remnant of the older population. They retained the old shoe of the Keftos. The new mode of Hellenic sandals was not there in evidence within a thousand years. Just as among the Karpathians, the upper part of the Kefto shoes was of white linen cloth with remarkable ornaments; these latter were sewed on with strips of different colors and were fastened by partially red and blue straps. The "stele of Ikonium" and the "gold cup of Vaphio" show in ancient times, the extension of the use of these shoes to the far north, especially in Europe.

The Sardinians and Etrurians living in the countries bordering on the western Mediterranean sea, according to Egyptian monuments in 1500 B.C., wore beak shoes. The shoes of the aboriginal Etrurians were shorter in the body than the usual beak shoes of the times. The shoes worn by the inhabitants of the

European Alps may have been derivates of the old Etrurian shoes. The Sardinian shoes are again seen in the reproduction of the ornaments of the silver bowl of Chiusi; the bowl itself may have been an Etrurian product of Cyprian style. The warriors wore high laceboots attached to high leathern gaiters. Many original Etrurian monuments show shoes very similar to the Kefto shoes, as evidenced in the bas relief of Cære. The high Sardinian laceboots, mentioned above, may have been retained as the native fashion of the population of the European Alps.

The Tyrolian singers, even to this day, wear these shoes and gaiters minus the curved beak. The soles of these shoes are doubled and are reinforced by iron nails, but contrary to the anatomic shape of the human foot, these shoes become narrow toward the toes. The Tyrolians maintain the style of lacing as practiced by their ancestors, but augment the covering with knitted woolen material which extends to the knees. We may safely conclude that the Europeans and many Asiatics, about 1000 A. D., wore wooden slippers and beak shoes combined, the former under the latter. Ultimately the wooden slipper, becoming a sandal, disappeared from the combination. The fight against imperfect and incorrect footgear is of long duration. The best possible was and is to try to mitigate the damage as much as this could and can be done. The history of beak shoes is as old as time. Whenever they were crowded out, sooner or later they were found to return and they persist to this very day.

Hellenic civilization drove the aboriginal people of the Kefto group, like the Pelasgians, to the country districts. The Hellenic idea was that the original shape of the human body constituted the highest degree of beauty. It was therefore shocking for a man of the education of Pericles to see people wearing beak shoes at the expense of the normal conformation and beauty of the foot. The Chinese and the Hellenic idea of beauty were directly opposed. A Greek artist could picture fools only as wearing beak shoes, were it not an offense esthetically to picture a fool at all. The Romans had no esthetic sense of their own. They were only obedient pupils of the old Greeks. Therefore, it is that the Greek and the Roman monuments furnish no contribution whatsoever to the history of the beak shoes. The reader will recognize the necessity of quoting from the early oriental monuments in order to furnish ethnographic history. Many thanks are therefore due the writer's old Nürnberg schoolmate, W. Max Müller, who is now Professor of Egyptology at the Pennsylvania University, Philadelphia, because of the help he has given in the presentation of this first complete history of beak shoes. Without his aid and his thorough knowledge of old Egyptian monuments, the task would have been next to impossible.

The high standard of esthetics faded out in the Byzantine period. Pictures of high Byzantine officers in native costume show that they wore shoes with long, narrow points; the foppery of the rustics was again victorious, absurd as this may seem.

The valleys and villages of Transylvania and Roumania are accessible only with difficulty. From century to century new nations and new populations migrated to the neighboring plains. There were atrocious wars, in consequence. Again and again were the old settlers extirpated by the immigrants. These new people in the next century met the same fate as those whom they had supplanted. These mountain fastnesses were the homes of the fittists among the Skythians, the Dacians, the Hungarians, the Bulgarians and other nations Their languages are now lost and but a few of their slang words are left to us—originally from the Ruthenic or the Roumanian tongue, the former of the Slavonic family, the latter of the Roman family of the Aryan group.

In these countries they still wear the old beak shoes and call them *botschcorn*. These *botschcorns* are a kind of leather sandal. They wear red socks and over them they fasten these sandals with their narrow curved points by means of straps. These sandals are also highly colored. In olden times there were Jews living among the Karpathians. These Jews were the prominent and intelligent men of the population. It is an historic fact that they refrained from wearing the botschcorn. They wore only high boots, as was customary among those living on the Russian plains. Although only sporadically used from 1000 to 1200 A D., beak shoes, from the twelfth to the fifteenth century A. D., were the mode of all Europe. They were primarily called Krakovian shoes and were doubtless replicas of the shoes worn in eastern Europe, the original home of the beak shoes. These shoes were without heels; only a second sole was sewed on. Later on, special wooden sandals, called in Germany *trippen* were worn contemporaneously with the beak shoe. The "trippen" are a shortened "ski." Later on, special heels were usual and still later on a kind of second heel was provided for the metatarsus pedis. "Trippen" was a very appropriate name because it means "noisy." The pedestrian wearing "trippen" made more noise than a convention of storks. At times the "trippen" were worn with a tiny bell attached to the toe part. The King of the Mardi Gras could not imagine shoes more grotesque than the beak variety of the 15th century; their very absurdity caused their early disuse.

### THE PREDECESSORS OF MODERN FOOTWEAR

For about 100 years the new mode of "duck beak" shoe remained in fashion. The toe end of this shoe was also non-anatomic on account of its narrow confines, but the upturned point was absent. After these "duck beak" shoes came the "bear paws" variety. Both of these kinds of shoes were heelless. The "bear paw" shoe was also styled the "cow mouth." The entire era was replete with innovations. The scientists renewed their study of the Greek language; the Reformers founded new religions; gunpowder was invented and in this period also America was discovered. Men of these times were not likely to overlook the need for practical footgear and they did not. And so it happened during this period that shoes with broad spaces for the toes first came into vogue. The celebrated men of all times have been honored in monuments as they have been sung in song. The inventor of the bear paw shoe should have been so recognized by his fellowmen.

Many of these celebrities were so honored, particularly during the 15th and 16th Centuries, and these supposedly life-like reproductions of the entire figure, invariably showed the bearpaw shoe. An instance of this can be found in the statue of Christopho Columbo in the circle at the junction of Eighth Avenue and 59th Street, in New York City.

Notwithstanding this healthy and common sense change in the style of footgear as it obtained in the 15th Century, there were frequent resurrections of the beak shoe. The Kilikians and the Assyrians, some time before Christ, wore shoes that were narrow at the toes, but without the upward curving point. Such was the oldest intermediary shoe between the beak and duckbeak styles. The modern shoe, as a rule, has the shape of the duck beak with the addition of a second or third sole and with a separate heel. Just as in 1500 B. C. the Kefto shoes had added soles, so there were similar shoes 1500 A. D. This can be demonstrated by a seal picture now in the possession of the Morgan Library of New York City, showing a Chetite (151 B. C.), wearing a beak shoe with a heel.

Separate heels bring the foot farther from the ground. The old Greek actors wore shoes with high heels; they were called Kothurns. The purpose was to increase their stature. The medieval trippen had heels and sometimes even double heels. In ordinary walking some parts of the shoe sole show early wear. If these places are reinforced by the application of a piece of leather, a starting point for a heel is created. The old Greek and Roman cities had very good pavements. In medieval times the pavement of cities and especially of small towns was extremely bad. This condition of affairs led to the use of shoes which prevented the pedestrian from sinking into the mud and dirt which was so common. In some sandy districts the people walked on stilts. The idea is the same as gave rise to the wearing of heels. The modern city is clean and has special sidewalks and accordingly the pedestrian of today does not require the same kind of shoes which were common in the medieval period.

The normal position of the feet in walking is horizontal. High heels make this position unnaturally oblique. The modern woman, however, likes to seem very tall and slender. She now wears very high heels on her shoes—higher in fact than ever seen in all the ages, and entirely unnecessary. With modern sidewalks and excellent roads, there is no excuse for such non-anatomic heels—it is purely an evidence of vanity which the common sense of the modern woman will probably shortly banish.

It would lead us too far to mention the high-shaft boots worn by the men and women of Russia and to comment on other kinds of footwear in use elsewhere. The above should be sufficient for a general genealogy of footwear.

Papyrus was the material of which sandals were made in ancient Egypt. This is desirable material as it will never cause corns or deformities of the feet. Such footgear, however, can only be used in flat countries with alluvial soft soil. Sandals would be useless in mountainous countries or where stones and thorns or snow and ice abound. In some countries foot coverings are and were made made of bark or of cork. Shoes of different kinds of cloths were, as now, in use. Very often the sole of the shoe was of leather, as is almost exclusively the case today in all large centres of population. Such shoes were worn by the Keftos about 1500 B. C., as has been previously stated. Shoes of felt provide a warm covering; they are today very much used in the home during the winter months. Rubber shoes protect against moisture. They are modern and are usually worn as overshoes.

The most common material for shoes are the skins of game and of cattle; such skins, however,' are very easily decomposed. The previous preparation of such skins is a measure of development of the time and of the nation. The natural hair can be used as a protection to the skin itself, as is common among the Finns. The surface may be prepared by fat or similar material to prevent the penetration of moisture. The best procedure is to make a homogeneous chemical compound of the albuminous matter of the skin. Such preparations are called leather. There are many different kinds of leather. That most commonly used is a chemical combination of albumin and some form of tannic acid. Different kinds of tannic acid are known to the botanic kingdom. It may be that in a later edition of this text book an augmented introduction of this subject as it bears on the botanic features of the question will be included.

To make good leathers requires time and patience. Some parts of the skin must be mechanically removed; other parts must be prepared by corrosion. It therefore, takes a long time before a sufficient cheimcal reaction between the skin and the tannic acid can be accomplished. North and South America have the best and the most skins; they also have the most and best vegetable tanning products. A good shoe can only be made of a good leather. The United States will continue more and more to supply the world with this product. Massachusetts is today the leader of the world in making shoes. But the manufacturers of shoes in the future will have to be more mindful of the hygienic features of their wares. The scientific podiatrist must help to have them establish this standard. It will be his part to insist upon their employing experts in tanning and in shoemaking. Thus the podiatrists can help to make the United States of America not only the greatest and the best, but the most sanitary shoemakers of the world. The writer realizes that this introduction to the history of Chiropody is a lengthy one, but it comprehends the scientific relation of the subject in detail and what follows will thus be more comprehensive.

### DENOMINATION OF HELOMA (CORN)

The scientific expression is heloma with the plural helomata; the common English expression is "corn." Almost every language and every period has a different word to express this common pedal woe. As Greek is the scientific language of the professions, "heloma" alone is scientifically possible. We shall see that the Greek physicians of ancient times used the word *helos* for corn and *tylos* for callus. Dr. Achilleus Rose, of New York, furnishes the writer with the information that the modern Greeks are now using only the old Greek word *tylos* to designate a corn, *tyloma* when speaking of a corn in its pathologic sense, and *tylosis* as the pathologic condition of existing corns. This information proves the condition there is the same as in other countries. It was not thought elegant to speak of such inferior profane things as corns; therefore, they introduced another word that should make a better impression; in this way, by disuse, they lost the original conception of the pathologic meaning of the word.

Modern scientific medicine paid little attention to corns. This neglect is clearly manifest. The minor consideration in which this subject was held may be shown by the formation of the absolutely unscientific word "papilloma." The formation of papilloma is linguistically unscientific. What papilloma is intended to comprehend is an absolute unscientific mixture, including skin tumors of all kinds as well as corns and their complications, a class of abnormalities thought to be too undignified for a surgeon's care.

The word papilloma comprehends different papillary tumors having external similarities such as condylomata, fibromata and carcinomata, accompanied by skin papillae. It is a bad scientific error to classify these tumors in a group with corns. But papilloma, as stated, is also linguistically incorrect. It is true that modern scientific medicine denominates all kind of tumors with the suffix *oma* in the singular, and *omata* in the plural. But this suffix is Greek and may only be affixed to Greek roots; *papilla* unfortunately is of Latin origin; therefore only an insufficiently educated man will use words like papilloma. *Papa* is an old reduplicated common Aryan word; but it is also found in many non-Aryan languages. It means father. A special Latin derivation is papilla; in the same way mamilla is derived from *mama* mother. The anatomist coins *mamma* (the female breast) from this root. Without sound displacement, many of the German family of languages also adopted these foreign denominations of father and mother. The united prominent excretory ducts of the mamma are called papillae. The characteristic elevation of the papillae of the mamma led to comparison with some pathologic products also arising over the level of the skin. A papilla is a very indefinite button-like elevation of the skin. A scientific podiatrist should use neither the word papilla nor the word papilloma in the manner now usually employed, because while the educated physician would be charged with carelessness for so employing these terms, the chiropodist would be accused of rank ignorance. The rich man may wear an Alaskan bead for a diamond; that would be a mere eccentricity on his part, but the poor man must wear the real stone or be charged with trying to impose on those about him.

The different nations have different popular expressions for corns. There is no common Aryan root for the word corn.

When the Aryans were still a single tribe, no shoes were known and no occasion arose for the acquisition of corns. Before shoes were known metal nails were invented. Wooden nails and metal nails are known from the tombs of the "Hallstatt" time and are also historic in the later "pile-work" period. The old Egyptians, Babylonians, Hellenes, Romans and Celts used nails, in the copper, bronze and iron ages. The northern nations of mountaineers, as well as the old Egyptians, used nails of hard wood. They were employed in buildings and other constructions and were especially useful in making warriors' shields. The metal nails of different sizes and shapes were made partly by casting and partly by forging. The nail heads, variously constructed as to size and shape, were used for ornamentation. In Homeric times, two kinds of warrior shields were known: *sakos* and *aspis*. They were made of layers of beef skin and their margins were metal-plated. The prominent nail heads in them were ornamentally arranged.

In the Anglo-Norman style of building, rhombic ornamentations constructed from and with nail heads are frequent types. In olden times these prominent nail heads were compared with the corn on the human foot. When the Aryans first designated foot, finger and finger nails, they were a single, united tribe without any offshoots. In subsequent years, when nails, shoes and corns came to be known, they were a divided family with numerous tribal subdivisions. No common root for the word corn was retained by the various members of this divided family, but there remained with all of them the idea of comparison of the corn with the head of a nail.

The old Greek physicians called the corn *helos* (ἦλος); the Latins of the same time termed the excrescence *clavus*; the Arabian physician, Avicenna styled it *al mismâr*. All of these designations have the primary dictionary meaning of "metal nail." This unity of idea is followed by the Germans who styled the wooden nails in use among them as *leichdorn*, the literal meaning of which is "thorn," or "wooden nail in the flesh."

To this day in lower Bavaria the popular treatment of a corn is to remove the "central thorn." In the Greek Attic language, *helos* (ἦλος) and in the Greek Doric language *halos* (ἆλος), both have the dual meaning of nail and corn. It is remarkable that this word is never used by Homer to mean to fix or to fasten, but only to designate the nail as an ornament; he uses the phrase "golden nail-heads." The old Greek naturalists and physicians employed the word *helos* to mean nail-head, wart, knot, callous on the hands or feet, also as a designation for pathologic tumors of animal as well as of plant life. Galenos and other leading physicians, however, used the word *helos* for the one purpose of designating corns.

The above outline, therefore, makes it clear that scientifically the corn should be known as *helos*. Pathologically it should be termed *heloma* (ἥλωμα), plural *helomata* (ἡλώματα), neuter gender. We speak, therefore, of an *heloma durum* as a hard corn, of *heloma molle* as a soft corn, plural *helomata dura* and *helomata mollia*. The condition of having an heloma or helomata is properly typified as *helosis* (ἥλωσις), female gender. Therefore, a patient may suffer from *helosis dura* or from *helosis mollis*, if he has an heloma durum or an heloma molle. The patient afflicted with *helosis* if a male, is an *heloticus* (ἡλοτικός), and if a female, an *helotica*. *Remedia helotica* are medicinal agents employed to relieve or to cure corns. They were so designated in medieval times. *Remedia anthelotica* or shorter *anthelotica* (ἀνθηλοτικὰ) would mean remedies banishing corns. *Helotomon* (the true Greek form) *helotomum* (an adopted Latin form) and *helotome* (English form), would be the knife with which corns are cut or removed. The word root is *temno* (τέμνω) meaning, "I cut." *Helotomos* in Greek and *Helotomus* in adopted Latin would mean one restricted to cutting corns. *Heliatros* would mean one limited to treating corns, just as *Podiatros* (ποδιατρός) is one limited to treating the foot, or (English) *Podiatrist*. Language makes the standard of nations and of individuals. Every language has elegant as well as ordinary expressions. The use of the above words, employed by well-equipped practitioners would eradicate the impression of the public as to the low standard of him whom they now term a "corndoctor"

We have previously referred to the German word *leich-*

*dorn*, meaning corn. The second part of the word *dorn* (English "thorn") is very well known. The first part of the word is noted in "lichgate," an English expression for "door of cemetery." The original English "lich" means the body, dead or alive. *Leichdorn* is, therefore, a thorn or a wooden nail in the body. Icelandian *likthorn;* Middle Low German *likdorn;* Swedish *liktorn;* Danish and Norwegian *ligtorn;* Hollandisch *liikdoorn.*

In High German, every well educated man would know the meaning of *leichdorn;* but in the ordinary spoken German of today nobody uses this word of his forefathers; and so too the English language has long since lost the original word "lichthorn," meaning corn.

The languages are continuously changing. The Latin language was the sole standard 2000 years ago. Now it is replaced by Italian, French, Spanish, Portugese, Roumanian and other Roman derivative languages. In the meantime we find Old French, Middle French and Provençalic. The transmutation of the living languages is accomplished as unconsciously as is the growing old of living people. New formed words insensibly replace old designations. Galenos and other old Greek physicians used *helos* as corn, but Dr. Achilleus Rose, who knows modern Greece and its Attic language, states that no modern Grecian would understand *helos* as meaning a corn. *Helos tu podos* (ἧλος τοῦ ποδὸς) meaning corn of the foot, would be clear to them although their usual term is *tylos* or more commonly *kalos* (κάλος). Both of these words in olden times meant callus and callosity. A corncutter in modern Athens is a *tyliatros.*

A like change and development may be noticed in almost every language which has any claim to antiquity. The Slavonic family of languages originally used the word *mosol* as meaning corn. Etymologists believe that this word is synonymous to the German word *maser*, which means a "knot in the wood." Here again, the idea of corns is the same as expressed in the German word *leichdorn*. *Mosòl* is the original word for corn in Russian and in Old Church Slavonian; Czechic *mozol;* Polonian *modzel*. The southern Slavonic languages, and the western ones as well, have entirely lost the old common word for corn. The Bohemians now call a corn *otlak* and the Polonians today term it *odcisk*. The first may originally mean only induration, the other surely does.

The expression *odciski u nog* or hardness on the foot, is surely forceful. An old Latin word meaning callosity is *callus*.

This word in the form *kalos*, previously mentioned, was doubtless borrowed from the Latin and is today the Greek slang word for corn. Callus has replaced the old Latin word *clavus* in all the Romanic languages of the southwest. The Portuguese dictionary gives *callo nos pes ou nas mãos*, as meaning callosities of the feet and hands. The first word of this quotation means corn. *Callo*, in the Spanish dictionary, is *dureza que se forma en los pies* or "induration formed on the feet".

In the French language *cal* and *callosité* mean simply callosity whereas *durillon aux pieds* is one of the expressions for corns, meaning hardness on the feet. Corns have many names in the Arabian languages. Arabic is now spoken in a very large district including many countries where in olden times only other Semitic and Hamitic languages were spoken. The Arabian has many dialects. Most of their root words are from the original of their own tongue, but they have borrowed much from their neighbors. Shoes were unknown to their early history—hence corns were equally unknown; they are the gifts of western civilization just as alcoholism was a present of the Whites to the American Indian.

Corn translated by *usuw*, is an Arabian expression meaning dry and hard. The inhabitants of Algiers speak Arabic, but are ruled by France. Pharaon and Bertherand noted there the use of the word *talula*, meaning corn; this seems only a mutilation of the French *durillon*. In another Arabian dictionary is found the word *thâlûl*, plural *thâlêl*, meaning corn. In the Syrian Arabian, a Jesuit reports having heard the word *kolkala* for corn; this latter may be a reduplication of *callus*. Most roots of the words of the Semitic languages have three consonants. Most of the derivatives are made by changing the vowels; prefixes and suffixes are only used in a restricted manner. It is quite impossible, therefore, to compound words in these languages.

The Arabian root *dâmal* means "to heal with a scar." Some pathologic words are derived from this root. *Damâl* is the black uredo of the blossom of the dates. *Dumäl* means *furnunculus* and *ulcus* and *dumâl* is a corn. *Demàn* as "corn" in Syria and in the Levant may be only a mutilation of the previous word. El Bochtor used this word. However, philologists have made and do make mistakes. Different Arabian dictionaries give *duhas* as *cor*, but the Arabian surgeons state *ulcus proveniens inter unguem et carnem, quo ille extirpari solet* which means "an ulcer between nail and flesh enforcing the extraction of the nail."

Everybody who studies the history of medicine must inevitably make errors if reliance for translations is placed on our own or on foreign dictionary misinterpretations. Every historian is therefore, invariably compelled to go back to the original source of the statements he finds. Many pseudo historians plagiarize the writings of their predecessors. In preparing the history of Podiatry it is at least pleasant to realize that the work is original and that no charge of plagiarism can possibly be laid at the door of the writer. Full credit will be accorded him for his work in this connection; so too he stands ready to shoulder any blame which may be charged against him because of inaccuracy of statements. It is hoped that nothing will be found here to be criticized.

We have mentioned how the aboriginal nations used the same term "corn" for the pathologic conditions as well as for the designation of nails and nail heads. We find there was also a second original idea because of which the same term was used indiscriminately for corns and for animal horns. Some nations had the impression that the corn was a horn or thornlike excrescence. If we take "lichthorn" in this sense and study the botanic embryology of the rose thorn in modern science, it will surprise us. For from this we will conclude that our forefathers had a very exact presentiment of the histologic development of the condition known as corns. In the same group of names there also belongs the word corn meaning the vegetable of that name. A study of medieval Latin shows that the origin of the word corn was not with them as we construe it. Provençalic was an old distinct Romanic language in the south of France. There corn was called *corne* and the same distinction, according to Fertiault, holds true today as evidenced in the dialect of the inhabitants of the city of Verdun. In modern French *cor* is the word for corn; time is probably accountable for the abbreviation. As stated above, all languages are continuously changing and these changes are particularly likely to affect the final seemingly superfluous letter or letters of a word.

The English word corn was borrowed from the French language, before the above abbreviation was effected. We find this English word first mentioned in an Anglo-Saxon medical book about 1000 A. D. In these old books, most medical words are from the Greek and Latin and are exactly as today. There the word corn is evidently used as equivalent to the Latin word *cornu* meaning horn and as also adopted by the intermediary French language. Some etymologists typify the pathologic word corn as heloma, in contradistinction to the vegetable corn; they evidently did not look up the medieval history of these words.

The vegetable corn is an English word of German origin. The corn of the United States is now largely a cereal which came from the aboriginal Indians. The complete correct expression would be "Indian korn." Corn in olden times in the United States and in the old country, as well, is about the same as rye. This word comes from an old common Aryan root. Here again we must consider the rule of sound displacing. The Latin equivalent for corn or for rye is *granum* meaning a granule. In ancient times and in the Orient even today, the druggists in weighing medicines, used barley granules. From this practice the apothecarists' weight was known as *granum* in Latin, *grain* in French and grain in English (formerly *gran* in German). The first Germanic derivative of this Aryan word for rye is *kaurno*, a change from *g* to *k* by the regular sound displacement as will be noted. This word became transformed into *korn* in all German languages and dialects such as Danish, Swedish, Icelandic and High German. The transformation into "corn" instead of "korn" is another illustration of the mutilations which typify many modern words. The root of the word corn of the foot is also Aryan and is common to all the languages of the Caucassian race. This root is a very old one and originally meant the horn of an animal. We find that this root is used in this sense in the different Semitic and Aryan languages. The Greek form is *keras* (κέρας), plural *kerata* (κέρατα), and is used to form the word *keratin*, which in modern Chemistry is an organic compound that is the basis of animal horns as well as a main constituent of the pathologic corn.

The original Aryan word "corn" has been transformed in the Germanic family of languages to *horn*. The Gaelic word for "corn," as used in Ireland, is *gart*. Whether or not this word is in any way cognate to the Greek *kerata* is not known to the writer. The Latin word *cornu* meaning "horn", retained the old "n" as the Hebrew *qeren* and the Arabian *qarn* and also the German *horn*. In Spanish the word for horn is *cuerno*. As above stated, the Latin word *cornu* meaning "horn" had also the meaning corn in the northwestern Romanic languages, as well as in the old Anglo-Saxon language. Shakespeare used the word correctly in Romeo and Juliet when he speaks of "a corn," but it is elsewhere intentionally mispelled as "coorne."

Words related to corn are found in the modern English language, partly from the Greek *keras* partly from the Latin *cornu* and partly from the English word horn. It would lead too far to give examples starting from the "rhinoceros" meaning "horn on the nose" to "greenhorn," a special New York kind of tenderfoot, to prove the varied uses of these various roots.

There is still another conception of the pathologic corn—this refers to their being considered as eyes. In old High German about 1000 years ago, corns were known as *hornin ouge* and *cornin ouge*, the one meaning "horn eye," the other "an eye of horn." These expressions were later on not understood and became by popular etymology the modern German *hühnerauge* which, literally translated, means "the eye of a chicken" instead as originally "an eye of horn."

Neither medical nor literary books show the use of this word in olden times. Grimm's Dictionary shows its earliest known use about 1501 A. D. Since that time *hühnerauge* predominates in High German and *leichdorn* gradually disappears. The physician, Leonhardus Fuchs, in 1583, explained the difference between the Greek words *helos* and *tylos*. In this treatise he states that the Germans usually call "corns" *hühneraugen*. The lower German districts retained the expression *leichdorn* for a much longer time, but there too this word has practically disappeared.

It may be that comparing corns and eyes is an old Turk-Tartarian idea. In Osmanli, the original language of the Turks, the corn was sometimes called *gözü*, meaning eye. Literally translated, the German word *hühnerauge* obtained entrance to branches of the Turk-Tartarian group of languages. Hungarian *tyúkszem* is a compound word of *tyuk* meaning hen and *szem* meaning eye. Another Osmanli or Turkish expression is *thawuq götü* from *thawuq* (hen) and *götü* (eye). In the Finnish tongue *varpaankänsä* means corn, which literally translated means "finger swelling." The expressions, *krähenauge, elsterauge egesternauge* and *agesterauge* of German origin, are also used to indicate the "corn." In the vulgar Arabian language of Egypt, made so from contact with their Turk-Tartarian conquerors, *ajun semek*, meaning fish eye (*ajun*, eye and *semek*, fish), is the expression for corn. The Aryan nations of the Baltic sea also mingled with the Turk-Tartarians. One of these nations, the Letts, designate corn as *wardazis, warshu azis* and *kunazs*. *Warde* and *kune* mean frog, and *azis* or *azs* means eye. The Lithuanian language is very similar to the language of the

Letts; there, *akis* means the eye and *wistakis* (literally, hen-eye) is their word for corn.

As previously stated, every language is undergoing continuous transformation. In these changes it is found that new words for corns are being constantly formed, and the old ones are being relegated to disuse or are brought forward for exceptional exhibition. In this connection there should be mentioned as additional Arabian words for corns: *bathrā fiālqadam* and *qarchā fiālqadam, silua* and *shutūna* Osmanli *nássir;* Scotch *bunyan;* English, "bunion." The word bunion may be derived from the Gaelic *buinne,* an ulcer; the old Swedish language had *bunga,* a tumor.

The Japanese call corns and callosities by the same name: *mame* or *uwo no me.*

### HISTORY OF THE PRACTITIONER OF CHIROPODY

There was no special profession of chiropodists in the past. In the last century the barbers very often practiced chirurgia minor, which comprehended chiropody. Barbers existed as such as far back as in the days of ancient Egypt. Material of the history of the Egyptian barbers is only completely collected from the Greek time and Karl Sudhoff of Leipzig has made this collection. They were not estimated as entitled to any standing. While they were subject to tax, the regular cosmeticians, including the perfumers, were taxed twenty times as much, which indicated that the comparative regard in which they were held was in that ratio. Even the smallest villages in ancient Egypt had at least one barber and usually many more.

Such work as corn-cutting was sometimes done by the barbers, sometimes by the surgeons and sometimes by the physicians. There were, in those days, specialists in operations for gravel and for stone and for eye cataracts and for other special conditions. Hellenic medicine made no progress in comparison with the old Oriental medicine of Babylonia and Egypt. The history of the world shows periods of distinct retrogression in scientific matters. In the prominent Hellenic cities, medical and priestly tutelage became disassociated. The difference between physician and surgeon in Greece persisted, but the physician ceased to be a priest and the surgeon remained in the class of artisans. Galenos, the Roman physician to the gladiators, wrote of both medicine and surgery. The collection of writings attributed to the name of Hippocrates also evidenced medical and surgical knowledge.

The Greeks first made use of the word *chirurgia*. This word is derived from *cheir* (χεῖρ), the hand. The Aryan languages contain no cognate words for hand. *Manus* and *hand* are respectively the Latin and the German equivalents. Literally, the words *chirurgia, manufactura* and "handiwork," express the same meaning, but in reality their application is quite different. All three words mean "a work by the hand," but the Greek *chirurgia* means a scientific work by the hand of one highly educated to perform it; this in turn means the surgical operation. *Manufactura* means an organized work by the hand of one highly educated for the purpose. "Handiwork" is work by the hand requiring no special education or cultivation. *Podagra* means gout of the foot; *chiragra* means gout of the hand; *chiromancy*, or more correctly *chiromantia*, is the foretelling of the future as gleaned from a reading of the lines of the hand. Chirography and chirology are also terms used in the English language.

As previously stated "chiriatry" is the only correct scientific expression for manicuring.

"Chirurgeon" is the old English denomination of surgeon. This word, originally from the Greek, was adopted by the Latins, by the French, and finally by the English. The second part of the Greek root *ergein* (ἔργειν) means "to work." The original Aryan root became the Greek word *ergein* and the English word "work," by the regular methods of sound development. In the English language of 500 years ago, the word was written "cirurgian"; Shakespeare wrote it "chirurgeon" and in the English of today it is written surgeon. The word chirurgos was used by Galenos and many old Greek authors in the sense of surgeon. In very ancient times the medical sciences were divided into three branches: magic medicine, pharmacotherapy, and surgery. In old English books the first is expressed as "witchcraft" and the second is styled "legecraft." The old common German word for physician was *laege*. It would have been correct to indicate in the formation of the word that the third (surgery) was really a handicraft but the surgeon disdained the idea of being a craftsman; hence the Greek word *chirurgus* or surgeon was adopted to designate him, who by his ability as a craftsman, plus his learning, was equipped to operate on the human frame.

Surgery that treats only of the foot, must have a special name. The most comprehensive and scientific designation of such a specialty was made of a combination of the words *cheir, pous* and *ergein;* chiropodurgia. This compound word means:

"The work of a man by the hand, on the foot." This word is too long; one would have to be free of asthma to pronounce it. In 1785 it was contracted to chiropodist. However, etymologically, this word is a monstrosity and is grammatically wrong. Chiropodist, literally, is one who uses the hands instead of the feet.

If one who makes the care of foot troubles a specialty were to go to Greece and to announce himself as a chiropodist, the educated Greeks might easily take him to be the chief clown of an up-to-date circus. The personal impression of the writer is that we should prevent the possibility of such a ridiculous misunderstanding by substituting the word "podiatrist" (physician of the foot) for the unscientific term "chiropodist." The term "chiropody" was first used in London in 1785 and later on in other cities and countries where English was the prevailing language. No other modern language accepted this word as evidenced by the fact that it is not contained in any of the dictionaries or encyclopedias of the German, the French, the Italian, the Spanish or other modern or ancient tongues.

It was left to the English language to accord a clownish name to one who should be really classed as a physician. The word "helotomos" would literally mean "corn-cutter" but the very fact that the word is of Greek origin presumes one who is scientifically educated as such. "Chiropodurgist" and the shortened "chiropodist," however, pretend and presume even more than the word helotomos implies. Heliatros means one who not only cuts corns, but who treats them in every regard. *Tyliatros* means the same in the modern Greek sense and is today used in Athens to signify what the English-speaking people call a chiropodist. "Podiatrist". literally means the physician who takes care of the whole foot. The word *podiatros* is used in modern Athens with just that meaning. In most modern languages chiropody is called "pedicure." This word and its derivates are also similarly used in the English language. "Pedicure" is also constructively incorrect and must therefore be considered unscientific; moreover the word is of Latin origin and no Latin word is or should be used to designate a scientific profession; in addition, the word is incorrectly compounded. *Pes* is the Latin word for "foot" and *curare* means to treat. The Greek language is able to combine such words, but the Latin is not. The word pedicure is therefore wrong and this may account for its minor use. *Le pédicure* or *le médicin pédicure*, is the French equivalent of chiropodist, *médicin* meaning physician; there is merit in this part of the designation. In German, the chiropodist is called *Hühneraugenschneider* or *Hühneraugenoperateur*. To a non-German the pronunciation of the word would be difficult. In Russia the chiropodist is known as *mosolnijoperator*.

The entire history of surgery is very fragmentary, but from these fragments we glean sufficient to realize that in ancient times in the Orient, surgery and chiropody were not separated. Magic medicine and pharmacotherapy were at times united, again they were separated. Surgery was only a member of this union in the classic times of the Greeks and the Romans; at all other times the surgeon had a separate profession. In medieval times it was unethical for the members of some medical faculties to have any consultation with a surgeon. Often the physicians were priests. The priests were forbidden to spill any blood or to come in contact with men or things befouled by blood. This superstition for almost five thousand years acted as an insurmountable barrier between medicine and surgery. The Greeks and Romans alone were free of this superstition. Scribonius Largus was physician to the wife of a Roman emperor and borrowed prescriptions from surgeons. Chiropody in olden times was a part of surgery or of the special "chirurgia minor" practiced by the barbers.

The education of the chiropodist seems to have been continuously the same from 3500 B. C. in the Orient to 1500 A. D. in the Occident, with very few variations. The apprentice was given room and board in the house of an experienced practitioner. He had to pay an apprentice's fee and had to make himself useful in various ways. Sons of other surgeons, especially if they were orphans, were absolved from paying the apprentice's fee and at times were provided with clothing, room and board. The apprenticeship was finished by a ceremonial commencement. There was usually a guild and a governmental supervision. The respective rights of the guild and of the government increased and decreased continuously. As a rule, a mixed commission gave the license. Sometimes the amount of knowledge, sometimes the amount of craft money decided the qualification for license. (Is it possible that the word graft came from craft?) A special history of the facts would be as tiresome as a century record of barometric motions. Most of the details we learn from the medieval free cities. There the candidate had to answer some scientific and some practical questions; but as recently as 1500 A. D. in Nürnberg, Germany, about fifty per cent. of these sciences was made up of astrologic superstition. At the commencement exercises the apprentice was subjected to a severe examination; the entire previous conduct of the candidate, his religion, his citizenship and his birth were all made subjects of inquiry. Even the question of the regularity of the marriage of his parents by a priest and inquiry as to their ancestors and the honesty of their acts were parts of this inquisitorial examination. Anything amiss in these details had to be equalized by cash payments made by the candidate or his father.

In the days of ancient and medieval Egypt the commencement exercises varied somewhat from those above recounted. The absolute monarch gave to one individual the power to decide as to the issuance of a license. The candidate therefore had to deal but with this one man. Prosper Alpinus described this Egyptian license craft very realistically. During this period arbitrary taxation was commenced.

The limits of the right of the surgeon for five thousand years were very undecided. As a rule, before or during or after a surgical operation, some medical treatment is necessary. In those days, and until comparatively recent times, the physician was not permitted to give this treatment because no consultation with a regular surgeon was allowed. Thus, by compulsion, the surgeons gained considerable experience regarding Materia medica. The physicians occasionally borrowed such prescriptions of surgical origin, as we learn from the writings of Scribonius Largus. Inasmuch as venesection or cupping was employed in almost all internal disorders, the surgeon treated practically all kinds of diseases. Thus, for instance, the surgeon was considered more competent to treat pneumonia than the physician. Operations for gravel and on the eye were known in the most ancient times. Proofs as to other operations in early history are lacking. The surgeon, as a rule, specialized only in one operation and travelled about from country to country applying his art. Possibly—we are not sure—corn cutting was in some periods just such a specialty.

The duties and qualifications of the average so-called surgeon in the ancient history of Babylon and Egypt were practically unlimited as to mechanics. In addition to their actual surgical work, the records show that there were surgeons who constructed buildings, built ships and managed quarries. Styled surgeons, these men were really mechanics. Engines were unknown in these times—handicraft was all that was available. When a great monument was to be erected or heavy bodies to be moved, the directing mind of the thousands of men employed in these undertakings was usually a surgeon. Their repute was such that their services were sought by and loaned to other countries. Such an instance occurred in 1500 B. C. when the king of the Chetites borrowed surgeons from the kings of Babylon and of Egypt. In the Babylonian language, surgeon is *azu* and in Egyptian *sunu*; the corresponding Hebrew word is *asa*. The Babylonian guild of surgeons invoked special protecting gods who were known as *Ninib* and *Gula*. The Catholic surgeons of medieval times had in the same way special patron saints. The chief Assyrian surgeon of the time of Assarhaddon and Sardanapal was Aradnanâ.

## SUPERSTITIONS OF THE OLD-TIME CHIROPODISTS

Plinius and Celsus were Latin authors; they collected many facts relating to ancient Oriental medicine. Their books are very important as tending to decipher the real sense of the fragmentary cuneiform and hieroglyphic records of ancient times. They probably however sifted out much of Oriental superstition as applied to medicine. Original Oriental surgery had on the one hand an exceedingly high standard of empiric knowledge but mixed with it an incredible amount of ridiculous superstition. In those days the science of medicine presented a general schematic rule of treatment. There was a main treatment of one day and a subsequent treatment of three days in Babylonia or of four days in Egypt. By this general rule we find that a corn-cutter must cut and subsequently burn out a corn on one day and must close the operated place by an ointment or bandage for three or four days. The facts were probably gained from experience, but superstition was so rife in those days that the practitioner led himself to believe that the rational did not apply to his work. The Greek physicians of Asia Minor, Hikesios, Asklepiades and Moschion, have preserved for us some of the old prescriptions of ointments to be applied after corn-cutting. These prescriptions are from the districts where beak shoes were first known and constituted what would even today be considered reasonable treatment. The ancient Orientals, especially the Egyptians, never attempted any task without making some remark relevant to the work in hand or of uttering a prayer or an invocation.

Just what formula was customary among the corn-cutters of those times is not known because neither records nor tradition tell. It is however known that the surgeons before operating were in the habit of saying: "Cutting may kill; but I hope to heal by cutting." Such was the custom 2000 B. C. The first-class surgeons in the succeeding centuries in doing their work amplified the above and used other sentences of similar import as well. About the time of Christ short sentences fell into disuse and in their place came lengthy incantations and prayers which were frequently obligatory. Infection often followed in the wake of unclean surgery and, as in those times there was no knowledge as to causes, it was common belief that something had been omitted from the incantation—a word or an inflection—and therefore it was that the devil had not been kept from doing his hellish deeds.

In the oriental times above mentioned, ammoniacal preparations were used as dressings for corn-cut surfaces. The influence of ammonia on keratin is known and the treatment thus employed must be conceded to have been reasonable. The only ammonia of ancient times was decomposed urine. It was popularly supposed that the urine of a special animal must be selected. For corns the old superstition sometimes required the urine of the ass. The ass was a symbol of a special god; in Babylon his name was *Nergal;* in Egypt *Set* and in Greece *Typhon.* It is possible to reconstruct by analogy almost the oldest incantation used in collecting this urine or in the after dressing; it was about as follows: "Fire threatens the operated foot; but god Typhon is pouring out an ocean between his legs. He refrigerates the wound, he extinguishes the spark." This and similar sentences are merely manifestations of the high religious sense of the surgeons of those times. They did not help and they did not damage; but after centuries of such practices, they created all kinds of superstition and lowered the entire scientific standard of medicine and surgery.

In very early times there existed another superstition which it would be well to here mention. Aboriginal mankind had no real calendar. The season was directly indicated by the varying positions of the sun in the zodiac; the time of day by the sun's position in the heavens. They well knew the influence of the moon to create high and low tide. They sought for the influence of stars on human life. This theory led to a long chain of superstition which firmly controlled the entire medical practice. This is known as the astrologic influence on medicine and surgery. This astrologic superstition is still alive among certain classes of people who are typified as civilized, and has a dangerous influence when employed to controvert efforts in behalf of the sciences. To this day we do not yet know the real limits of the influence of seasons, of daylight and of darkness in relation to the development and manifestation of certain diseases. On these undecided boundaries the superstitious still fight the real sciences and often the results are discouraging. In most cases, however, the reasonable man can easily recognize the unreasonable superstition. Such superstitions led to all sorts of humorous situations. Thus, for instance, at one time it was thought unholy and therefore unlucky and even dangerous, to operate on given days; again, it was not permissible to cut a nail on the same day that a corn was cut and vice versa; again the nails of the hand were not to be cut on the same day that the nails of the toes were cared for and vice versa.

From the above it will be noted that what the modern Schools of Chiropody teach today, even though it delves into the scientific realms heretofore sacred to the practicing physician and surgeon only, is much less taxing than was necessary to the practitioner of bye-gone centuries. The latter had to burden his mind with the study of all features of witchcraft and superstition and of contemporaneous and preceding experience, all of which involved a mental study which was as confusing as it was exacting. It was empiricism pure and simple, plus the supernatural. Today it is science, pure and unadulterated.

All of the superstitions, as such, mentioned in the preceding paragraph were the practices of the times previous to 3500 B. C. Through the kindness of J. W. S. Johnson, of Kjöpenhavn, Denmark, the writer has recently received a reprint of the licensing examination of chirurgus minor in the year 1500 A. D. in the city of Nürnberg, Bavaria. If the language of the latter were not regular German and if the very frequent allusions to the religion of the time were not Christian, no expert historian would be able to decide between the methods employed 3500 B. C. and 1500 or maybe 1700 A. D. This applies equally to the intermediate time in China, India, Babylon, Egypt and western Europe, including Germany. The astrologic superstitions were potent through all this time in the consideration of chirurgia minor.

Empiric knowledge and astrology were continuously the main bases in chiropody and in other surgical practice. There was, however, no stability about these practices and superstitions; they varied from time to time as do the winds. About 700 B. C. in Assyria these superstitions were but idle factors, but about 650 B. C. they became all-powerful.

The reader can hardly expect a long list of chronicled data of these fluctuations through the five thousand years. Sometimes the priests had the secular power; in these periods the medical superstition was not so pronounced, but when an imperialistic king ruled by military despotism, superstition, as a rule, ran rampant. It would perhaps be well to here relate the effect of astrologic superstition as it influenced the study of Anatomy and Physiology. In olden times the body was supposed to consist of hard and of soft parts (bones and flesh). Their idea was that the blood circulation consisted of two systems of tubes: the veins, which contained moving blood, and the arteries, which contained mobile air. The esophagus was to their view a vein and the trachea was an artery. The venous system started in the liver and the arterial system began in the nose. Sweat (perspiration), urine and mucus of the nose were to their thinking, end products of impure blood. All the hair of the head, of the beard, of the axilla, of the genitals, as well as the nails of the fingers and the toes, were emitted rays of arterial air, and the latter was called "pneuma." The highest degree of impure pneuma was generated in hair lice, in fleas and in other parasites. They believed that the urine must be voided some time, but they had a similar notion regarding the mucus of the nose. They thought it necessary to cut the hair and nails. The female sex was believed to be freed from this rule— they were moist— and thus it was decreed that hair-cutting was necessary for the male sex only. Some countries and periods assigned a higher value to the so-called pneuma, others considered the blood itself of most importance. The smooth shaved Egyptian priests were advocates of the greater importance of the pneuma. The Jewish priests on the other hand were believers in the theory that the blood should be given the preference and therefore did not shave at all. Each held the other as unclean, as can be learned in the story of the Egyptian Joseph.

The four constituents of the living body were, to their minds, parallelisms to the four Empedocles elements (fire, water, air and earth). All the events in the body, in the state and in the stars of the heavens, were believed to be parallelisms, one ruling the other, but themselves all controlled by an unknown central ruler. This central ruler was a god or a family of gods in a very much fettered condition. The entire world, including the stars, were the makrokosmos and the human body was the mikrokosmos. Every part of the body was ruled by a special zodiac sign or by a special planet. The arms were ruled by the twins and the feet by the fishes. Starting from the new moon, every surgical operation was prohibited on the 7th, the 14th, the 19th, the 21st and the 28th day. Operations on the hands were forbidden for two or three days of every month if the moon was in the zodiac sign of the twins; operations on the feet were prohibited in the same way during the moon's position in the fishes. Operations on tissues were only allowed when the moon was in crescent; tumors should be exsected only in the decrescent moon. Therefore, toe nails could be cut only in the time of the crescent moon and corns were operable only in the decrescent moon. It was thus permitted to cut corns for but ten or eleven days every month. It was very difficult to decide on what day an ingrown toe nail should be operated upon. It is the opinion of the writer that in such a case a careful corncutter had to call in five or six experts to determine the days proper for such a procedure. It is more than likely that it was customary to take two different days to complete this operation; the incarnated part of the nail having to be cut off in the decrescent moon.

The modern scientist laughs while reading of these strictures, but some centuries ago it was a very serious matter. Neglect of any of these rules was malpractice. The code of laws of king Hammurabi of Babylon, 2200 B. C., states: "A surgeon guilty of careless operation will have his hands severed from his body." It is certain that the corn-cutters of those days preferred to conform to the then-existing code rather than run the risk of having this condign punishment meted out to them.

The astrologic idea led to a careful study of all kinds of individual variations in the tissues of the body. They tried to draw conclusions as to the character of the patient and as to his future. There was also much superstition employed in this study. As Dr. Naecke of Hubertusburg, Saxony, stated, criminal anthropology today successfully collects and draws conclusions from body abnormalities.

In the time of cuneiform writing the scientists studied not only all abnormalities of the feet, but also the abnormities of the nails. Long ago they recognized the fact that no two individuals have identical nails. They used an impression of the five nails of the right hand as an absolutely sure identification of the owner. In Babylon and in Assyria the finger and nail imprint was generally used for individual signature and seal. An expert was able in every instance to unqualifiedly identify such a signature or seal.

In the district pervaded by so-called Babylonian culture, the captives of war were ofttimes mutilated. They had no modern ideas of humanity. People guilty of offense against the laws were also mutilated. They destroyed the eyes, they cut the ears, they maimed the nose, they cut the female's breasts, they maimed the hands and the feet of the guilty ones in keeping with their offenses. Usually that part of the body which was used in committing the crime was singled out for punishment. We learn these facts not only from their code of laws but also from pictures in bronze which show some of these acts of punishment. We learn from the gospel that it was a common practice of the Kanaanitic nations to cut the thumbs and big toes of war captives. Such acts led to much experience in operations on the feet and toes. It is therefore, not to be wondered at if in those days of empiricism and superstition there was still a high standard in connection with operative work on the feet.

There was one particular superstition which constituted a most serious handicap to the surgeon of the times: in astrology, the planet Mars ruled the metal iron and the planet Saturn presided over the destinies of lead. Mars and Saturn were supposed to be bad planets, harbingers of death; from Mars a quick death, from Saturn a slow death. Therefore, in ancient times it was not allowed to bring any iron or lead in contact with a surgical wound. The weapons of warfare in ancient Rome were of iron because the Romans thus wished to poison their enemies. The same idea accounts for the use of leaden gun balls in medieval times. The mutilation of enemies and of those guilty of crime was permitted by means of iron and of lead, but both iron and steel were prohibited in the form of surgical instruments. Gold and silver were too expensive. In very remote times knives of flint stone were used. Dr. Lewi recently told the writer that he had heard of a case in very recent years, where in China operations on corns had been performed by means of sharpened flint stone. This is confirmatory of the known persistence of astrologic superstitions among the residents of Eastern Asia. Metal surgical knives were in olden times made of copper. In the Hammurabi period such copper instruments were used. In the Roman period knives were principally of bronze.

### HISTORY OF THE SURGICAL AND MEDICAL TREATMENT OF CORNS

The surgical and medical treatment of corns cannot be older than when corns were first notably in evidence, which means that their treatment is contemporaneous with the earliest use of shoes.

The earliest chiropodists, however, quickly acquired experience of a high order in the treatment of these affections and their knowledge was passed on from one generation to another. As a matter of fact there has been but very little that is new in this connection excepting during the past few years. Bloody excision of the corn was one form of treatment, but years ago the bloodless operation for entire excision of the corn was successfully practiced by the knife as also by means of plasters and cataplasms. A newer treatment is by means of pressure to the corn by an adjusted ring.

The Egyptian text books of medicine contain no treatment of corns, probably because of the fact that the ancient Egyptians did not wear shoes. In the Babylonian districts we properly suppose that corns were the subject of study and of treatment. About a thousand pieces of medical cuneiform inscriptions belonging to the library of king Sardanapal of Assyria and a smaller number from other places are left to us. Since the writer commenced this chapter, a large number of tablets containing cuneiform inscriptions relating to medical matters have been unearthed by a German expedition. Very few of these have been thoroughly studied.

The Babylonians had special chapters on every minor subject and also on every kind of illness. Among these medical relics there are many general text books, in which the pathology of every part of the body is specifically classified and systematized. A large tablet contains special details of the pathology of the foot. It was excavated about 1850, but has not yet been edited. Another text book is entitled "The Large Veins." It is very much mutilated. The fourth line of this text book contains the sentence: "The foot is painful." Possibly this book may relate to varicosity of the foot. It contains fourteen pages of cuneiform text, but no scholar has as yet been sufficiently interested to thoroughly decipher these mutilated pages because on its face it is quite evident that it deals almost exclusively with superstitions. The treatments consist of incantations and superstitious ceremonies. These texts were copied in Assyria about 650 B. C., at a time of pronounced superstition in that country. In those days they may have been afraid to cut corns. Incantations were certainly safer for the surgeon than was the use of the knife; because of these former he could never have his hands cut off for malpractice. So it will be seen that the incantation treatment for the removal of corns was a form of faith treatment in vogue long before the days of Mrs. Eddy and even before the Christian era.

Susruta, a physician who lived in India long years ago, wrote a medical textbook. We have no exact data to show just when Susruta lived but his book is written in the old Sanskrit language. One part of this book is called Chikitsitasthána, which means therapy. In the 18th subdivision of this part of his work he recommends that all smaller, non-malignant and non-purulent tumors be totally extirpated. A contraindication for this treatment arises when the growth is in the neighborhood of a joint. The bleeding after extirpation was appeased by cauterization. If a corn was inflamed and suppurating, the tumor was opened by a small (surgeon's) knife and cleaned with a special liquid; thereafter it was covered by a soft ointment. The basis of this ointment was a mixture of honey and butter. If no suppuration was present, an oil preparation was recommended. Embelia ribes, Bignonia indica and Indigofera indica were boiled in this oil. In old India also there were many people who were afraid of a knife in the hands of an operator. Many different ointments were employed in such cases. Urine, which is extemporized ammonia, sesam oil with an alkali, which is extemporized soap, and other applications are advised in Susruta's work for the local treatment of growths and tumors of all kinds. It is only occasionally that Susruta advises surgical and pharmacotherapeutic treatment, whereas in the time of Sardanapal, as a rule treatment by incantation was practiced.

From antiquity to the most recent times every period promiscuously employed surgical, pharmacotherapeutic and superstitious methods in the treatment of corns, but one or the other was always the favored treatment. Why, even in these days the Christian Scientists pray for the relief and removal of a corns and just as we know that this treatment is not scientific, so a majority of the people at one time implicitly believed that incantations were not only scientific, but thoroughly efficacious, whilst the use of the knife was distinctly unscientific.

There are many special chapters in the Papyrus Ebers, Papyrus Brugsch, Papyrus Hearst and in the Magic Papyrus of London on the pathology and therapy of the feet. Sometimes they advised local treatment, sometimes they prescribed internal treatment, because their writings show that even five thousand years ago in Babylon and in Egypt they recognized that while some affections of the feet are purely local conditions, others are symptoms of an affection of the general system.

On the walls of a tomb of very ancient times, Professor W. Max Müller of Philadelphia found what is very probably the oldest picture relating to the care of the feet, a copy of which is here reproduced.

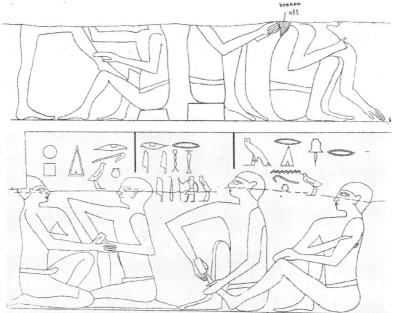

THE OLDEST EGYPTIAN PICTURES RELATING TO THE CARE OF THE FEET.

The care of the feet was also known in the earliest times of Greece. In the songs of Homer, Erykleia washes the feet of

ERYKLEIA WASHES THE FEET OF ODYSSEUS.

Odysseus. A very old picture is found in Gomphoi which is also here reproduced.

There were other civilized nations along the borders of the eastern Mediterranean sea before the time of the Greeks. The university of Turin, in Italy, has in its possession a figure of terra cotta, which represents a woman cleaning her foot. This is pre-

A CYPRIOTIC TERRA COTTA SHOWING A WOMAN CLEANING HER FEET.

Homeric and is part of the material which the Italian, Cesnola, excavated in the island of Cyprus. Of the old Greek authors, Theophrastus and Dioscurides make mention of corns; the latter was a physician of Anazarba. Hikesios, a physician of Smyrna and a follower of Erasistratos, who lived about 100 B. C., prescribed a specially long plaster for the treatment of corns. His methods were followed by Asklepiades, a physician of Prussa. in Bithynia, about 70 B. C., and a few decades later by Moschion Hikesios, Asklepiades, Moschion and Dioscurides were born in Asia Minor, where beak shoes were worn. The history of corns also started there and there too special corn plasters were first devised.

This text book of Chiropody is an entirely new publication and

all of the matter contained in it must necessarily be bibliographically original. Modern text books treating of branches of science that possess a bibliography are often largely copied from books previously written on the same subject. A twelfth book is frequently but a compilation of what was contained in the books written by the eleven preceding authors. In this manner the corn plaster of Hikesios was imitated by Kriton, and Kriton in turn was imitated by Herodotus, and the latter furnished Galen with the means of treating his patients.

If, in this chapter, the writer were to copy a given prescription, more than likely some manufacturing chemist would in turn compound the preparation, patent it and quote the approval of physicians throughout all the centuries of its use. In this manner, Celsus and Plinius, in Latin, and Galenos, in Greek, created their respective text books. The treatments advised by Celsus were largely gleaned from Oriental sources. Plinius collected his data from all known nations and, although in the main he mentions the sources of his information, some of his so-called original matter is again copied.

In the first century after Christ, all kinds of treatment of corns were employed. The bloody and the bloodless operation were common; preoperative pharmaceutic and postoperative pharmacotherapeutic treatment were known; local ointment or plaster applications, without operation, also had vogue and the superstitious were not behindhand in devising methods of all kinds for the cure of corns. If one were to collect and publish all of the corn cures which were utilized during the first century of the Christian era, this entire volume would not be sufficiently large to contain the data.

Of the later Greek physicians, Aetios, in his "Tetrabiblion," recommends the radical bloody operation as the only treatment for corns. He calls the forceps used by the corn-cutter "volsella" and the knife "oxykorakon."

The Arabian physician Avicenna, who flourished at a later period, does not make himself clear as to his methods of treating corns. He employs the same word for a tumor of the female uterus as he uses for designating corns. He does not recommend surgical treatment for paronychia, corns and similar disturbances; he invariably, and without exception, prefers local applications for all of these conditions.

ᚠᛁᛋ ᚹᚫᛖᛋ ᚻᚩᚱᛋᛖ ᚠᛁᛟ ᚠᚩᚾ ᚦᛖ ᚻᛁᚹ ᛒᛁᛟ ᚳᛟᚱᚾ ᚩᚾ ᚠᚪ ᚠᛖᚳ.
ᛋᛖᚾᛖᚩᚾ ᛋᛖᚾᛖᚳᚾᚩᚾ ᛋᛖᚾᛁᚳᚢᛚ ᚳᚪᚳᚪᛚᚩᚾ ᚳᚪᚾᛖ ᚳᚻᛁᚱᚳ ᛈᚪᛒᛁᚱᚳ. ᛖᚳᛗ ᛁᚠ ᚠᚩᚾ
ᚾᚢᚾᛖ ᚾᚪᚻᚳ ᛁᚠ ᚠᚩᚾᚾᚢᚾᛖ. ᚾᛖᛋᚢᛁᚠ ᚪᚾᚾᚢᚪ ᛗᚪᚾ ᛁᚠ ᚠᚳᚪᚾᚪ ᚾᛖᛋᚢᛖ ᚳᚪᚾᛟᛟ.

The oldest known corn cure of England is in reality a horse cure. This is reproduced in Leechdoms, Wortcunning and Starcraft of early England. It means in Anglo-Saxonian: "This maeg horse with thon, the him bith corn on tha fet," or English: "This may cure a horse, that has a corn on his feet." The cure in this case is only an incantation and the incantation is not a homogeneous one. It begins by referring to seven Greek words with alliteration; that is, three g's, three c's and one p. The words are very much mutilated and constitute merely an allusion to the birth of Christ. The second part is Anglo-Saxon: "etm is forrune, naht is forrune," or English: "The breath is run away and the night is run away." Similar sentences are very common in medical incantations, meaning that sickness should disappear as something that never returns, if once gone, such as the human breath or the night. The third part is in Latin and, like the Greek part, is very much mutilated. Restored, as it is known from other manuscripts, it means: "You (the corn) cannot return next year and also not later on." This Anglo-Saxon incantation to a corn shows that medieval medicine and surgery were absolutely influenced by the Greeks and Romans. As we have learned, they in turn acquired it from Asia Minor.

Our researches show that in medieval times pamphlets of a hygienic character were prepared for travellers. The care of the feet is there emphasized. In all of these books no original matter is found—the text is entirely made up of extracts and compilations. There was, in these times, a strong prejudice against the new, and therefore innovations were not to be expected. About 1500 A. D., Bartholomæus Maggius wrote a pamphlet on the treatment of gunshot wounds. This certainly was original matter, but the author sought to escape the charge of originality by attempting to prove that Hippocrates, who lived two thousand years before the author, would have treated these gunshot wounds in just such a manner as indicated. If such new research work was dangerous for the recognized physicians and surgeons of the time, it may readily be concluded that an innovation in the treatment of corns was even more dangerous to the then practitioners of chiropody—the barbers.

The movement therefore to treat corns and kindred diseases of the feet in a scientific manner is absolutely a new departure.

Joannes Tagaultius, 1555, *Gesner, 1555, Leonardus Fuchs, 1583, mention the treatment of corns. It would perhaps not be difficult to find that about one hundred other physicians of this time wrote on the subject of corns but always in the same way, without originality, without scientific data and quoting merely the collective experiences of the writers among the physicians of the first century after Christ. It is of course important that we should know the methods employed in these olden days if only to keep far away from the empiricism and the superstition which prevailed. Since then, the medical sciences have made great progress. Especially great have been the advances in surgery since a full knowledge of antiseptics, X-ray diagnosis, radium therapy and other features of treatment have come to our knowledge.

Modern scientific podiatry must utilize all modern progressive methods. Continuous progress by continuous comparison with the old and the very ancient methods may lead to the same high standard as the cosmeticians won for themselves in the time of queen Kleopatra. But this high modern standard should calculate on creating the Podiatrist as a specialist in medicine—one who should stand in the front rank of the cosmeticians. The chiropodist of yesterday is the podiatrist of today; he now has his own professional School of Chiropody and his own scientific text book. The text book of Cosmetics, written by queen Kleopatra, as previously stated, is lost; it may never be resurrected. Those who are to write future volumes bearing upon the subject, here presented in large detail, should bear in mind that this effort on behalf of the School of Chiropody of New York is in keeping with the scientific spirit which created the School and which would now create a literature for podiatry worthy of the cause.

*The numerous writings at this time, even though of old material, were probably due to the fact that at this period the wearing of the Beak Shoe had practically ceased. However, the fear of foot troubles from their use still remained.

[The writer of the preceding pages wishes to express his gratitude to Dr. M. J. Lewi, the editor of the Text-Book, for his valuable services in aiding him to properly present the matter contained in this Chapter in the English language.]

CPSIA information can be obtained
at www.ICGtesting.com
Printed in the USA
LVHW081232090822
725497LV00004B/121